If Only He Knew

Other Books by Dr. Gary Smalley

For Better or for Best

Hidden Keys of a Loving, Lasting Marriage

Joy That Lasts

If Only He Knew

A Valuable Guide to Knowing,
Understanding, and Loving Your Wife

•••

DR. GARY SMALLEY

ZONDERVAN BOOKS

ZONDERVAN BOOKS

If Only He Knew
Copyright © 2012 by Gary Smalley

Published in Grand Rapids, Michigan, by Zondervan. Zondervan is a registered trademark of The Zondervan Corporation, L.L.C., a wholly owned subsidary of HarperCollins Christian Publishing, Inc.

Requests for information should be addressed to customercare@harpercollins.com.

ISBN 978-0-310-59932-6 (audio)
ISBN 978-0-310-59931-9 (ebook)

Library of Congress Cataloging-in-Publication Data
Smalley, Gary.
    If only he knew : a valuable guide to knowing, understanding, and loving your wife / Gary Smalley with Steve Scott.
      p. cm.
   ISBN 978-0-310-32838-4 (softcover)
    1. Marriage—United States. 2. Marriage—Religious aspects—Christianity. 3. Wives—United States. I. Scott, Steve, 1948- II. Title.
   HQ734.s684   2010
   248.8'.425—dc22   2010043329

All Scripture quotations, unless otherwise indicated, are taken from the *New American Standard Bible®*. Copyright © 1960, 1962, 1963, 1968, 1971, 1972, 1973, 1975, 1977, 1995 by The Lockman Foundation. Used by permission. (www.Lockman.org).

Scripture quotations marked NIV are taken from The Holy Bible, New International Version®, NIV®. Copyright © 1973, 1978, 1984, 2011 by Biblica, Inc.® Used by permission of Zondervan. All rights reserved worldwide. www.Zondervan.com. The "NIV" and "New International Version" are trademarks registered in the United States Patent and Trademark Office by Biblica, Inc.®

Scripture quotations marked KJV are taken from the King James Version. Public domain.

Any internet addresses (websites, blogs, etc.) and telephone numbers in this book are offered as a resource. They are not intended in any way to be or imply an endorsement by Zondervan, nor does Zondervan vouch for the content of these sites and numbers for the life of this book.

Cover photography: David Arky/Corbis®
Interior design: Katherine Lloyd, The DESK

Printed in the United States of America

24 25 26 27 28 LBC 62 61 60 59 58

CONTENTS

A Note from the Author's Wife 9

If Only I Knew 11

1. HOW TO DRIVE YOUR WIFE AWAY WITHOUT
   EVEN TRYING 13

2. WHERE HAVE ALL THE FEELINGS GONE? 31

3. IF YOUR WIFE DOESN'T WIN FIRST PLACE, YOU LOSE! 47

4. YOUR WIFE NEEDS YOUR SHOULDER, NOT YOUR MOUTH . . . 63

5. CLIMBING OUT OF MARRIAGE'S DEEPEST PIT 79

6. WHAT NO WOMAN CAN RESIST 111

7. ASK HOW YOU CAN IMPROVE AS A HUSBAND 121

8. IF YOUR WIFE'S NOT PROTECTED, YOU GET NEGLECTED . . . 131

9. ARGUMENTS . . . THERE'S A BETTER WAY 145

10. A SUCCESSFUL MARRIAGE . . . IT'S EASIER THAN
    YOU THINK 159

11. SO YOU WANT A PERFECT WIFE 171

12. WATCH OUT! IT CAN HAPPEN TO YOU 187

Resources 191

To the number one woman in my life,
Norma Jean,
and to our children,
Kari, Greg, and Michael

A NOTE FROM THE AUTHOR'S WIFE

It has been over thirty years since Gary first published *If Only He Knew*. It's hard to believe Gary and I have been working with couples for the past forty years. Now in our seventies, we have much to look back on and much to be thankful for. Of the fifty-plus books Gary has written, *If Only He Knew* still gets the greatest volume of feedback. We get letters and emails on a regular basis from couples thanking us for the help that this book has been to them.

In our continuing work with couples, Gary and I have come to one conclusion: There is no such thing as a unique problem. In fact, most couples are usually relieved to know their problems are common to many, if not all, couples. Because marital problems can be so similar, if you find a solution that works with several couples, it usually will be effective for most couples.

Please rest assured that you are not the first husband in the history of humanity to experience the problems you are facing. The principles that Gary shares in this book have not only made our marriage more fulfilling, but they have had similar results in the lives of countless other couples with whom we have worked. As you begin to apply these principles to your relationship, you should begin to experience a deeper and richer marriage.

Norma Smalley

IF ONLY I KNEW

Before I approached Gary about writing a marriage book for men, I knew his material was good, but I had no idea how meaningful it would be to me personally. After all, I had been married for almost ten years and I was nearly an ideal husband ... I thought. As I began to work with Gary on the material for this book, it became more and more clear that I was not a successful husband by any stretch of the imagination. I was providing for my wife's material needs and some of her physical needs, but that's where it stopped.

As I got deeper into the content, I realized that for years I had been unaware of many of my wife's emotional needs. For years, she had to put up with a husband whose callousness and indifference forced her to suffer through day after day of not having her deeper needs lovingly satisfied. I am extremely grateful for all that I have learned in the past two months. At last my eyes have been opened, and I see my wife as the unique, beautiful individual that she really is. I am devoting the rest of my life to becoming the husband she deserves. The content of this book not only opened my eyes to my wife and her needs, but it gave me concrete ways to meet those needs. If you get one-tenth the value from this book that I have gleaned from its pages, it will be the most valuable book you'll ever read about marriage.

Steve Scott

1

HOW TO DRIVE YOUR WIFE AWAY WITHOUT EVEN TRYING

■ ■ ■

You husbands in the same way,
live with your wives in an understanding way.

1 Peter 3:7

At the other end of the phone a quivering voice said, "You've got to help me. She has a court order against me." George was coming to me for help after his relationship with his wife was already in shreds. "We've been married over twenty years, and she won't even let me back in the house. I can't believe she would treat me this way after all I've done for her. Can you help us get back together?"

Before I answered his question, I wanted to talk to his wife.

"There's no way you can talk to Barbara," he said. "She wouldn't talk to you. The moment you say you're representing me in any way, she'll hang up on you."

"I've never been turned down by a wife yet," I assured him, "so we might as well see if this will be the first time. Would you give me her phone number?"

To be honest, as grim as things sounded, I did wonder if she would be the first wife not willing to talk to me about her marital strife. But my doubts were unfounded—she was more than anxious to discuss their problems.

"What would it take for you to be willing to let your husband back into your life? What would have to happen before you would try to rebuild a marriage relationship with him?" Those were the same questions I had asked many wives who claimed they didn't want their husbands back.

Her response was typical. "I can't possibly answer that question. He's the worst husband in the world, so I wouldn't think of taking him back. I can't stand his personality or his offensive habits anymore." The court order would take care of him, she told me. "Just keep him away!"

I gently asked her if she could tell me the things he had done to offend her. When I heard her response, I said, "It sounds like he hasn't been a very sensitive and gentle husband, has he?"

Once again I asked her to stretch her imagination and think about what changes would be necessary before she would take him back.

There was plenty of room for improvement, she told me. First, he was too domineering and critical of her. Second, he tried to control her every move with a possessive grip. Third, he trampled her sense of self-worth with constant ridicule. And fourth, although he always had time for business and other interests, he seldom took time to listen to her. On top of all that, he spied on her and didn't give her any freedom.

"Don't get any ideas, though," she told me at the end of our conversation. "Because no matter what, I won't stop the divorce."

When I relayed these complaints to George, I knew I had touched some sensitive spots. He defended himself and accused her. I let him rant for a while before asking, "Do you want your wife back?"

"Yes, I'd do anything to get her back," he said.

"Good. I'm always willing to work with someone ready to re-adjust his life. But if you're not totally serious, let me know now. I don't like to play games." Again he committed himself to change, but his commitment didn't last beyond my next statement. "We're going to have to work on your domineering and possessive nature. It shows you don't genuinely love your wife."

He fumed, spouted, defended, and fought so much I began to wonder if he really would commit himself to the necessary changes.

"I've never met a more belligerent, stubborn man in my entire life!" I exclaimed.

Suddenly subdued, he responded, "That's not my nature. I'm usually rather submissive inside. Maybe I'm putting up a front because I'm really not a pushy person. I feel like people run all over me."

"I don't think you and I are talking about the same person," I responded. "If I were your wife, I'm not sure I could bear up emotionally under your domineering personality."

That stopped him long enough for him to give our conversation some serious thought. After talking to his friends and even praying that God would help him understand, he returned to my office able to confess his faults and ready to change.

"If you really want to love your wife, then you need to begin right now, at the divorce trial," I said. Now that we were on the subject, he mentioned that he needed to get a lawyer because she had one.

"No," I cautioned him. "If you want to win her back, you need to forget about a lawyer this time." (I don't always recommend this, but based on their personal background, I felt he would stand a better chance of regaining her love without legal counsel.)

"You're crazy," he said. "They'll take me to the cleaners."

Feeling somewhat defenseless, he reluctantly agreed to forfeit legal counsel.

Two of his friends and I waited in the courthouse for the closed-room session to end. He came running out of the courtroom bellowing. "She wants 20 percent of my retirement ... 20 percent! No way I'm gonna do that!"

Once again I asked him, "Do you want your wife back?"

Again he nodded yes.

"Then give her 25 percent," I told him. I reminded him that *now* was the time to respect her and treat her sensitively. Later, he emerged from the courtroom a divorced man, but not for long ...

Several months later I ran into him at the grocery store. "My wife and I remarried," he said triumphantly. "I thought you were crazy when you first told me the things I should do for my wife ... there was no way I would ever be able to do them. It took sheer willpower at first. I only did them because you said that God rewards those who seek him and follow his ways. But you know, it's really amazing. After doing them for three months, I actually enjoy them."

He continued to give examples of the new ways he was treating his wife. Like the time she took a business trip and he wrote her a note telling her how much he wished he could be with her. Inserted in the note were extra money and directions on how to reach her destination.

George has finally realized that his wife is a special person who needs tender treatment, almost as if her forehead were stamped "Very Important—Handle with Care."

He has discovered the secret to renewing any strained relationship—honor. But before we discuss rebuilding a failing marriage, let's examine two major reasons marriages fail.

High Expectations and Limited Training

The first reason marriages fail is that we tend to enter marriage with storybook expectations and limited training.

I once asked a college student what kind of man she would like to marry. "I'd like for him to be able to tell jokes, sing and dance, and stay home at night."

"You don't want a husband," I told her. "You want a television."

Her visions of a husband reveal one of the most common reasons marriages fail. We marry with unrealistic expectations and few, if any, caring skills. In fact, most of us are rather fuzzy when it comes to our mate's real needs or desires.

Isn't it ironic that a plumber's license requires four years of training, but a marriage license requires nothing but two willing bodies and sometimes a blood test? Since most of us bounce through the educational corridors without any basic communication courses, many men marry with absolutely no knowledge of how to build a meaningful relationship. In short, most men have no idea how to love their wives in a way that makes both of them happy.

I once asked five divorced women, individually, "If your husband began treating you in a consistently loving manner, would you take him back?"

"Of course I would," each replied. But, unfortunately, none of them had hope that her husband would ever be like that.

Because I knew one of the men personally, I had to concur with his wife's hopelessness. If he were willing to try, he could win her back. Unfortunately, he wasn't interested in learning.

"What he doesn't realize is that most women are as responsive as puppies," one woman told me. "If he'd come back and treat me with tenderness, gentleness, and understanding, I'd take him back tomorrow."

How sad that we men don't know how to win our wives back or even how to keep from losing them. How can we win their affection, their respect, their love, and their cooperation when we don't even know where to begin? Instead of trying to learn what it takes to mend a cracked marriage, most of us, out of desperation, jump on the divorce bandwagon.

We violate the relationship laws inherent in marriage, and then we wonder why it all goes sour. But we wouldn't wonder if the law of aerodynamics sent a one-winged airplane plummeting to the earth.

Imagine yourself an aerospace engineer working for NASA. Your job is to put several people on the moon, but something goes wrong halfway through their flight. You wouldn't dream of walking out on the entire project because something went wrong. Instead, you and the other engineers would put your heads together, insert data into the computer, and ... voilà! You would work night and day to try to discover the problem and make all the vital adjustments to get that spacecraft back on course or help the astronauts return to earth. If the project had failed altogether, you still wouldn't forsake it. You would study what happened and modify it to avoid similar problems in the future.

Like the spacecraft, your marriage is subject to laws that determine its success or failure. If any of these laws are violated, you and your wife are destined to crash. However, if during the marriage you recognize which law or principle you are violating and make the necessary adjustments, your marriage will stay on the right course.

Ignorance of the Differences between Men and Women

I would venture to say that most marital difficulties center around one fact — men and women are different. The differences (emotional, mental, and physical) can be so extreme that without a *concentrated effort* to understand them, it is nearly impossible to have a happy marriage. Freud once said, "After thirty years of studying women, I ask myself, 'What is it that they really want?'" If this was his conclusion, just imagine how little we know about our wives.

You may already be aware of some of the differences. Many, however, will come as a complete surprise. Did you know, for instance, that every cell in a man's body has a chromosomal makeup entirely different from those in a woman's body? How about this next one? Dr. James Dobson says there is strong evidence indicating that the "seat" of the emotions in a man's brain is wired differently than in a woman's. By virtue of these two differences alone, men and women are miles apart emotionally and physically. Let's examine some of the differences between men and women.

Mental/Emotional Differences

1. Women tend to be more *personal* than men. Women have a deeper interest in people and feelings—building relationships—while men tend to be more preoccupied with practicalities that can be understood through logical deduction. Men tend to be more conquest oriented—competing for dominance—hence, their strong interest in sports such as football, boxing, and NASCAR.

Why would a woman be less interested in a boxing match? Because close, loving relationships are usually not developed in the ring! Also, watch what happens during many family vacations. He is challenged by the goal of driving four hundred miles a day, while she wants to stop now and then to drink coffee and relax and relate. He thinks that's a waste of time because it would interfere with his goal.

Men tend to be less interested in and knowledgeable about building intimate relationships, both with women and with other men. For example, women are the primary consumers and readers of marriage books. They are usually the ones who develop the initial interest in knowing God and attending church. When a man realizes that his wife is more naturally motivated to nurture relationships, he can relax and accept these tendencies and *choose* to develop a better marriage and better relationships with his children.

As a husband, do you realize that your wife's natural ability for developing relationships can actually *help* you fulfill the two greatest commandments taught by Christ—loving God and loving others (Matt. 22:36–40)? Jesus said that if we obey these two commandments, we are fulfilling *all* the commandments. Think about it. Your wife has the God-given drive and ability to help you build meaningful relationships in both these areas. God knew you needed special help because he stated, "It is not good for the man to be alone. I will make a helper [and completer] suitable for him" (Gen. 2:18 NIV). If you let her, your wife can open up a whole new and complete world of communication and deeper relationships.

2. Women become an intimate part of their surroundings. Dr. Cecil Osborne, in his book *The Art of Understanding Your Mate*, said women become an intimate part of the people they know and the things that surround them; they enter into a kind of "oneness" with their environment. Though a man relates to people and situations, he usually doesn't allow his identity to become entwined with them. He somehow remains apart. That's why a woman, viewing her house as an extension of herself, can be hurt when it's criticized. A man may not realize it, but when he yells at the kids for something they did, his words affect her deeply as well.

Women tend to find their identity in close relationships, while men gain their identity through vocations.

3. Women often need more time to adjust to change. Because of a woman's emotional identity with people and places around her, she needs more time to adjust to change that may affect her relationships. A man can logically deduce the benefits of a change and get psyched up for it in a matter of minutes. Not so with a woman. Since she focuses on immediate consequences of relocating, for example, she needs time to overcome the initial adjustment before warming up to the advantages of it.

4. Women tend to express their hostility *verbally* whereas men tend to be more *physically* violent.

Physical Differences

Dr. Paul Popenoe, founder of the American Institute of Family Relations in Los Angeles, dedicated his most productive years to the research of biological differences between the sexes. Some of his findings are listed below, along with their effects on us.

- Women have greater constitutional vitality, perhaps because of their unique chromosomal makeup. In developed nations, women normally outlive men by four to eight years.
- Women's metabolisms are usually lower than men's, making weight control more difficult for women.
- Women's bodies have several unique and important functions related to childbearing: menstruation, pregnancy, and lactation. Their bodies release more of the hormone oxytocin, which is related to bonding and empathy.
- Men produce more testosterone, which is related to aggression, focus, independence, and drive.
- Women's blood contains more water and 20 percent fewer red blood cells. Since the red blood cells supply oxygen to the body cells, women tire more easily than men. For example, when the working day in British factories was increased from ten to twelve hours under wartime conditions, accidents increased 150 percent among women, but not at all among men.
- On the average, men possess 50 percent more brute strength than women (40 percent of a man's body weight is muscle, while muscle is only 23 percent of a woman's body weight).

There are many more examples, of course, but even these few differences underline how the physical differences between men and women can cause strife in a marriage. A man who expects his wife to have the strength and endurance that he has is not only ignorant but foolish. And a woman who resents her husband's focus and drive to succeed is fighting against his basic biological nature.

Sexual Differences

A woman's sexual drive tends to be related to her menstrual cycle, while a man's drive is fairly constant. The hormone testosterone is a major factor in stimulating a man's sexual desire.

A woman is stimulated more by touch and romantic words. She is far more attracted by a man's personality, while the man is stimulated by sight. A man is usually less discriminating about those to whom he is physically attracted.

While a man needs little or no preparation for sex, a woman often needs hours of emotional and mental preparation. Harsh or abusive treatment can easily remove her desire for sexual intimacy for days at a time. When a woman's emotions have been trampled by her husband, she is often repulsed by his advances. Many women have told me they feel like prostitutes when they're forced to make love while feeling resentment toward their husbands. However, a man may not be aware of what he is putting his wife through if she feels he is forcing sex upon her.

These basic differences, which usually surface soon after the wedding, are the source of many conflicts in marriage. From the start, the woman has a greater intuitive awareness of how to develop a loving relationship. Because of her sensitivity, she is initially more considerate of his feelings and enthusiastic about developing a meaningful, multilevel relationship: that is, she knows how to build something more than a sexual marathon; she wants to be a lover, a best friend, a fan, a homemaker, and an appreciated partner. The man, on the other hand, does not generally have her instinctive awareness of what the relationship should be. He doesn't know how to encourage and love his wife or treat her in a way that meets her deepest needs.

Since he doesn't have an understanding of these vital areas through intuition, he must rely *solely* upon the knowledge and skills he has acquired *prior* to marriage. Unfortunately, our educational system does not require a training program for a husband-to-be. His only education may be the example he observed in his home. For many of us, that example may have been insufficient. We enter marriage knowing a lot about sex and very little about genuine, unselfish love.

I am not saying men are more selfish than women. I'm simply saying that at the outset of a marriage most men are not as equipped to express unselfish love or as desirous of nurturing a marriage into a loving and lasting relationship as women are.

Differences in Intuition

Norman was planning to invest more than fifty thousand dollars in a business opportunity that was a "sure thing." He had scrutinized it from every angle and had logically deduced that it couldn't miss. After signing a contract and delivering a check to the other party, he decided to tell his wife about the investment.

Upon hearing a few of the details, she immediately felt uneasy about the deal. Norman sensed her uneasiness and became angry, asking why she felt that way. She couldn't give a logical reason because she didn't have one. All she knew was that it just didn't "sit right." Norman gave in, went back to the other party, and asked for a refund. "You're crazy!" the man told him as he returned Norman's money. A short time later, all of the organizers and investors were indicted by the federal government. His wife's intuition had not only saved him fifty thousand dollars, but it may have kept Norman out of jail.

What exactly is "woman's intuition"? It's not something mystical. According to a Stanford University research team led by neuropsychologists McGuinness and Pribran, women do catch subliminal messages faster and more accurately than men. Since this intuition is based on an unconscious mental process, many women aren't able to give specific explanations for the way they feel. They simply perceive or feel something about a situation or person, while men tend to follow a logical analysis of circumstances or people.

Now that you know some of the differences between men and women, I hope you will have more hope, patience, understanding, and tolerance as you endeavor to strengthen and deepen your relationship with your wife. With this in mind, let's look at some of the serious consequences of allowing a poor marriage to continue its downhill slide.

Serious Consequences of a Poor Marriage

First, a woman desires love from her husband. A poor marriage can cause a woman to develop any number of serious physical or mental ailments requiring thousands of dollars' worth of treatment. If your wife is seriously depressed, overweight, or constantly coming down with the latest bug, one cause of her problem may be a poor marriage.

Second, when a husband mistreats his wife, their sex life will suffer. To make things worse, the man then might turn to adultery or porn to meet his sexual needs and may find himself trapped in addictive behaviors that are extremely difficult to overcome without extensive counseling.

Third, a husband's lack of love for his wife can drastically affect their children. Like their mothers, children might suffer physical or mental illness as the result of a poor marriage. Rebellious children are more likely to be found in the home of a man who does not know how to lovingly support his wife. And because children model themselves after their parents, their future marriages are in danger of suffering the same negative patterns that they witnessed in their parents' marriage.

Fourth, when a man settles for a poor marriage, he is forfeiting his reputation before all the world. He is saying, "I don't care what I promised at the marriage altar; I'm not going to try any longer." By refusing to love his wife as he should, he is telling those around him that he is self-centered and unreliable.

The Hardest Change You May Ever Make

I am not trying to force you into the "perfect husband" mold. I don't know *any* perfect husbands. However, I do know some who are learning how to respond to their wives' special needs.

I do want to help you learn how to love your wife more effectively and consistently. At first you may feel like you're learning to walk all over again. Weeks, months, or even a year may pass before you reach your goal of consistent loving behavior. After you learn to make progress, you will gain confidence. Soon you will be right in the midst of the kind of marriage you never thought possible.

Remember—you may feel it's impossible to change lifelong habits, but it's not. It usually takes four to six weeks to change a habit. So I hope you will decide to try to change yours. For some men it may take the accountability of a small group or the support of a pastor. However, I know from experience that the rewards are well worth the effort.

The Secret to a Fulfilling Marriage

What is the secret of a fulfilling marriage? Hard work and persistence! Sometimes in the middle of a conflict with Norma I really want to give up. But that's only how I *feel*. Often I'm tired, run down, under too much stress—consequently, the future looks bleak. That's when I rely upon knowledge, not feelings. I act upon what *will* strengthen our relationship, and in a few days I see the results. In fact, I usually feel better the next day and have renewed desire to work on our marriage. So I never give up. No matter how I feel, I keep acting on the secrets of lasting relationships that I've learned from the Bible.

Remember, *you* are the one who gains when you strive to have a loving relationship with your wife. My wife has told me dozens of times that when I treat her well I'm the one who wins. My loving care motivates her to do extra things for me, to respond gladly to my needs and desires, but her response has never been my main motivation. The strongest motivation for me has been the *challenge* and *rewards* of living my life as outlined in Scripture. For me, it's following the two greatest teachings of Christ—to know and love God and to know and love people (Matt. 22:36–40). All the joy and fulfillment I have desired in this life have come from these two relationships—with God and with others (Eph. 3:19–20; John 15:11–13).

These relationships are so important that I added to my life another motivation—perhaps the best motivation for me. I allowed a few other couples to hold me accountable for loving my wife and children. They have the freedom to ask me how we're doing, as a couple and as a family, and I know they love me enough to lift me up when I fall. And I always try to remember that love is a *choice*. I choose to care about my relationships. That same choice leading to great rewards can be yours.

My wife and I have committed the remaining years of our lives to the study of skills needed to rebuild meaningful relationships. I have personally interviewed thousands of women about what actions of their husbands tear down or build up their marriages. Basically, this book is a summary of my findings. Even now, some thirty-plus years from the first draft of this book, we have ministered to over a million men worldwide, calling them to an all-out commitment to their families.

Your wife may be a career woman without children or a busy homemaker and mother of three. Whatever the case, I believe you can *customize* the general principles in this book to build a more fulfilling relationship with her.

Before reading the next chapter, take this short marriage checkup quiz to determine how healthy your marriage is at this time. Then, when you have pinpointed your strengths and weaknesses, read the rest of the book, taking the steps that are necessary to strengthen your relationship. Some of the ideas for this checklist are from Dr. George Larson, a psychologist who has done extensive work helping people develop good relationships. He believes, as I do, that good relationships don't just happen. They evolve and are sustained only when people know what they want and how to get it.

Marriage Checkup Quiz

1. Do you make your wife feel good about herself?

(yes _____ no _____)

2. Do you value the same things in your wife that you value in yourself?

(yes _____ no _____)

3. Does your face spontaneously break into a smile when you see your wife?

(yes _____ no _____)

4. When you leave the house, does your wife have a sense of well-being, having been nourished by your company?

(yes _____ no _____)

5. Can you and your wife tell each other honestly what you really want instead of using manipulation or games?

(yes _____ no _____)

6. Can your wife get angry at you without your thinking less of her?

(yes _____ no _____)

7. Can you accept your wife as she is instead of having several plans to redo her?

(yes _____ no _____)

8. Is your behavior consistent with your words?

(yes _____ no _____)

9. Do your actions show you really care for your wife?

(yes _____ no _____)

10. Can you feel comfortable with your wife when she's wearing old clothes?

(yes _____no _____)

11. Do you enjoy introducing your wife to your friends or acquaintances?

(yes _____no _____)

12. Are you able to share with your wife your moments of weakness, failure, or disappointment?

(yes _____no _____)

13. Would your wife say you are a good listener?

(yes _____no _____)

14. Do you trust your wife to solve her own problems?

(yes _____no _____)

15. Do you admit to your wife you have problems and need her comfort?

(yes _____no _____)

16. Do you believe you could live a full and happy life without your wife?

(yes _____no _____)

17. Do you encourage your wife to develop her full potential as a woman?

(yes _____no _____)

18. Are you able to learn from your wife and value what she says?

(yes _____no _____)

19. If your wife were to die tomorrow, would you be happy you had the chance to meet her and to marry her?

(yes _____no _____)

20. Does your wife feel she's more important than anyone or anything else in your life other than God?

(yes _____no _____)

21. Do you believe you know at least five of your wife's major needs and how to meet those needs in a skillful way?

(yes _____no _____)

22. Do you know what your wife needs when she's under stress or when she's discouraged?

(yes _____no _____)

23. When you offend your wife, do you usually admit you were wrong and seek her forgiveness?

(yes _____no _____)

24. Would your wife say you praise her at least once a day?

(yes _____no _____)

25. Would your wife say you are open to her correction?

(yes _____no _____)

26. Would your wife say you are a protector, that you know what her limitations are?

(yes _____no _____)

27. Would your wife say you usually consider her feelings and ideas whenever making a decision that affects the family or her?

(yes _____no _____)

28. Would your wife say you enjoy being with her and sharing many of life's experiences with her?

(yes _____no _____)

29. Would your wife say you are a good example of what you would like her to be?

(yes _____no _____)

30. Would you say you create interest in her when you share things you consider important?

(yes _____no _____)

If you answered "yes" to *10 or fewer* questions, then your relationship is in major need of overhaul.

If you answered "yes" to *11–19* of the questions, your relationship needs improvement.

If you answered "yes" to *20 or more* questions, then you're probably on your way to a good, lasting relationship.

For Personal Reflection

1. What two main responsibilities are required of every husband? See 1 Peter 3:7.

2. What is the biblical requirement to love? What do these verses have in common: John 15:13, 1 Corinthians 13:5, and Philippians 2:3–8?

3. What do we gain from loving others? See John 15:11, Galatians 5:13–14, and Ephesians 3:19–20.

2

WHERE HAVE ALL THE FEELINGS GONE?

■ ■ ■

But the greatest of these is love.

1 Corinthians 13:13 NIV

"I don't love you anymore," Sandi said casually, shocking Jim out of his intense interest in a baseball game on TV. "I want to leave you, and I'm taking Jamey with me."

Since Sandi and Jim believed themselves to be sensible, educated adults, they separated calmly and agreed on a settlement without dispute. Jim, in his "maturity," even helped Sandi pack. Then he calmly watched as she and his daughter left his house for good. But he wasn't calm on the inside. He couldn't keep food down for the next month, and it wasn't long before he developed shingles and boils. His physical problems were only symptoms of a much deeper problem—a lack of *knowledge* and *interest* in building a lasting marriage relationship.

Fortunately, Jim was able to win his wife back with genuine love. It took a year, but Sandi was finally convinced by the changes in Jim that their marriage deserved another try. Jim got a second chance at his marriage. Unfortunately, not all men do.

Just what did Jim learn about love during a year of separation from Sandi? He learned that a successful marriage, like any other worthwhile endeavor, takes time, intention, and study.

Who would think of allowing an untrained man to climb into the cockpit of an airplane and tinker with the gauges? Or who would allow a novice to service the engines of a modern jet? Yet we expect men to build strong, loving relationships almost without any education at all. Great marriages require great education. You first must discover the essentials of genuine love, then practice them until those skills are sharp and natural. Soon your awkwardness will give way to masterful ability.

Remember the couple I mentioned in the first chapter? By the time George finally asked me how he could win his wife's love back, she had already obtained a court order to keep him away from the house. The divorce was pending, although he desperately wanted to salvage their marriage of many years. I can remember telling him, "It'll be difficult. But I assure you, as long as she isn't in love with another man, what I'm going to share with you will work."

At first, he felt awkward using the techniques I shared with him. He had to begin at zero and slowly learn to talk to Barbara, to be tender, and care about and understand her feelings. He didn't know her special needs, that she longed for comfort and not lectures when discouraged. But in time, he did learn, and he did win back his wife. He said he couldn't believe the gestures that once felt so awkward were now an enjoyable part of his life.

For example, most men who did not grow up in warm, loving

homes tend to struggle with hugging. For these men, hugging can feel uncomfortable. Yet I have made it one of my missions in life to teach aloof men how to be warm and learn how to hug. What at first feels awkward becomes second nature for many men who keep at it. The same is true of just about any marital skill.

"It's just not worth it," one husband said when I told him how to save his marriage. "Don't you see, I don't like her anymore. She bugs me, and I don't even want to make the effort to build what you're talking about. I just want out."

"What's the matter between the two of you?" I asked, trying to find out why his love for her had vanished. "Why can't you extend yourself toward her and try to build a loving relationship? Why don't you want to?"

"Well," he confided, "several things she has done have hurt me so much that I just can't try anymore."

The next day at lunch he named seven things his wife had done, and continued to do, that made him feel like leaving. To his amazement, we were able to trace each area he hated in his wife to an area he saw lacking in his own life. Once he understood this, he asked, "What kind of man would I be to dump her when I'm contributing to what I dislike about her?"

A marital relationship that endures and becomes more fulfilling for both the husband and the wife is no accident. Only hard work makes a marriage more fulfilling five, ten, fifteen, or twenty years after the honeymoon. I enjoy my wife's company more than ever, and I've been married for over forty-five years! And do you know what? It gets easier on most fronts, but I confess, it still takes effort to stay in unity, harmony, and oneness. We're still learning and practicing more and better ways to live in a win-win relationship. There's no such thing as finally reaching a place of total relaxation and just letting the relationship slide. There will always be work involved, but it's more than worth it for not only my own health, but also for Norma's well-being.

The Three Essential Kinds of Love

Nearly every man enters marriage believing his love for his mate will never fade. Yet in the United States, for every two couples who marry, one will divorce. Why? Because we have believed in Hollywood's version of love. But it doesn't take long to discover that mere passion, which revolves around sexual gratification, is not sufficient in itself to establish a lasting relationship. Unfortunately, too many couples begin their marriages thinking this type of love is all they need.

There are at least three kinds of love, each unique. Of the three—affection, passion, and genuine love—I believe only genuine love provides an adequate foundation for a secure relationship. If a relationship lacks genuine love, it will most likely deteriorate. One of the most exciting virtues of genuine love is that it can be developed within your character without the help of affectionate feelings. Before we look at genuine love, however, let's first consider the other two types of love.

Affection

Here we're talking about the "I like you" feelings we have toward the opposite sex—the kind of love that pleasantly stimulates all five senses. She smells good, feels good, sounds good, and looks good. She is pleasant company because she makes you feel happy. You love her like you love pizza or you love country music.

Many relationships begin with this type of love. We all notice attractive features in others. Soon we find ourselves enjoying the parts of their lives that make us feel good. We get to feel strong rewards just by being with them.

Though this love is the foundation for many marriages, it doesn't always withstand the pressure of time. After two or three years, the wife changes her lifestyle and hairstyle while her husband opts for new cologne and different political views. The older they get, the more they change.

We all change to some degree each year. The danger arises when we base our love on changeable characteristics we found attractive on the affection level. Our feelings grow colder and colder until finally we wonder what we ever liked about our mates in the first place. So we're off to look for someone new to love. We miss those old "reward feelings" when we're with her. It's easy to see why affection love has trouble maturing and lasting over the years.

Passion

Passion works harder on the emotions than affection. It's the type of love that keeps the heart working overtime: "Hey, you really turn me on!" The Greeks called it *eros*—a sensual and physical form of love that often produces ardent physical involvement before and after marriage. Eros love heightens our senses and stimulates our bodies and minds. It's the kind of love that hungers for the other person to stimulate and satisfy our sexual urges. This love is certainly found in marriage, but if passion exists without genuine love, usually lust gives way to disgust and repulsion, as it did with King David's son Amnon, who hated Tamar after he raped her (2 Sam. 13:15).

Genuine Love

Genuine love is completely different. It means, "I see a need or desire in you. Let me have the privilege of assisting you in meeting it." Instead of taking for itself, genuine love gives to others. It motivates us to help others reach their full potential in life.

Most important, genuine love has no qualifications. It doesn't say, "I'll be your friend if you'll be mine." Nor does it say, "I want you to be my girlfriend because you are beautiful and I want people to see us together," or, "I want to be your friend because your family is rich." This love does not seek to gain, but only to give. Don't you remember those junior-high crushes when you said, "Well, I'll like her if she likes me, but if she gives me a bad time, I'm dumping her." Genuine love has no such fine print.

Some time ago I found one of the secrets to remaining in this type of love. It's honor. I decided to highly value my wife, holding her in high esteem. Other than God himself, I honor and value her more than anyone or anything else in this life. She is my treasure, and as Jesus noted, "Where your treasure is, there your heart will be also" (Matt. 6:21 NIV).

The Lowest Level of Maturity

The ability to love in a selfless way is dependent upon your level of maturity. The emotions listed below are typical of immature love. Check the ones characteristic of your life.

☐ *Jealousy* is caused by a fear of losing something or someone we value because it or they meet our needs.

☐ *Envy* springs from a desire to possess what someone else has. We imagine that if we gain what he or she has, then we'll be happier.

☐ *Anger* results from the inner turmoil and frustration we feel when we cannot control people or circumstances. We cannot have what we believe will make us happy or our goals are blocked.

☐ *Loneliness* results from a dependence on other people for our happiness.

☐ *Fear* results when we imagine or perceive that our needs or goals will not be met.

If you want to continue this exercise, you should make a list of incidents that have triggered each emotion you checked. Then ask yourself, "Why did I feel the emotion? Was I focusing on what I could *get* out of life or what I might *lose* in life?"

All these emotions are characteristic of immature love — a desire to use other people for personal happiness, a hunger for pleasure without regard for the cost. This same immaturity is behind the abuse of alcohol, drugs, and sex and the weakening of all our relationships.

The Highest Level of Maturity

I believe the more we help others achieve their full potential in life, the closer we are to maturity. Demonstrating a selfless desire for others to gain is the strongest base for building lasting relationships. How can you go wrong when you develop a love that is primarily concerned with building a deep and lasting marriage? Or you have a love based on identifying your wife's specific needs and then looking for creative ways to meet them? This kind of love cannot fail!

Take Her Viewpoint into Account

What do you think is the major stumbling block for most husbands in developing a lasting love for their mates? I have found that it is failing to meet a woman's needs or desires from *her viewpoint.*

When Anna told him she felt unloved in certain areas, Mike was dumbfounded. "What do you mean?" he asked her.

"Well, for years you have been a great husband and a very helpful person, and you've done a lot of nice things for me," she explained gently. "But sometimes you do things I don't need. I'd appreciate it if you'd find out what is important to *me.*"

A man's brilliant idea for showing love can backfire. Like the time I decided to have our house painted as a special surprise for my wife. What was special to me wasn't so special to her. Although she appreciated the paint job, she would have much rather had a new kitchen floor. When I realized that, I stopped my projects long enough to buy her a new kitchen floor. Then we made a list of priorities from her point of view. They were quite different from mine!

By the way, when you use your energy to satisfy your marriage relationship from *her* point of view, you'll find that your wife will bend over backward to try to make you happy. Thousands of wives have told me, "When I see my husband making me first place in his life, caring for my deepest relational desires, I can't wait to do the same for him." So don't stop treating her well for fear that she won't return the favor. If you are consistent and persistent in your loving deeds, she eventually will.

Doing things for others *our* way is a selfish, immature form of love. My heart goes out to those wives who have received pool tables for Christmas, tickets for a trip to the fishing swamps of Louisiana, or invitations to the Motorman's Ball.

If you've never done so, find out what *your wife* needs to feel fulfilled. Then look for special ways to fulfill her needs. At first she may not believe your caring attitude will last. Don't despair. It takes a long time to develop a sturdy relationship.

Many wives are cautious at first when they see their mates becoming more caring. Like the joke about the husband who went to a lecture on marriage, then surprised his wife at their front door with a huge hug, a box of candy, and a dozen roses. "Oh, this is terrible," she said, weeping. "The baby cut his finger, I burned your dinner, the sink is stopped up ... now *you* come home drunk!"

Don't be surprised if your wife doesn't understand your actions at first. It took at least *two years* before Norma could see the changes in me after I promised her that I would start loving her better. Now she knows I am committed to spending the rest of my life developing our relationship and getting to know her new needs as they change.

Learning how to love your wife in a mature way is like raising a productive vegetable garden. Our first year in Texas, we decided to grow a vegetable garden. After we dug a small plot, I dumped nearly half a bag of fertilizer on it and let it sit for three months to be sure I'd have a lush garden. But something went wrong. When the carrots came up, they were a little brown around the edges. All the tomatoes began to rot on the bottom before they ripened, so we had to pick them while they were green. None of our beans survived above the half-foot level, and our cucumbers bit the dust.

I was truly puzzled until an expert gardener told me I had "burned" my vegetables with too much fertilizer. My intentions were good, but my knowledge was limited. If only my vegetables could have talked. If only the beans could have said, "Hey, you up there! You put way too much fertilizer in this garden, and we're having a tough time. The chemicals are killing us, and if you don't do something about it, we're all going to die." If my vegetables could talk, I could have the world's greatest garden.

A husband can fail in much the same way if he doesn't know exactly how much of each "love ingredient" his wife desires. Fortunately, unlike vegetables, my wife can talk. I can ask her just *what* she needs, *how much* she needs, and *when* she needs it.

(Wives, if you are reading this, let me assure you that we as husbands generally *do not* know what you need. So we ask you to help us learn by telling us your needs in a gentle, loving way. Let us know when we aren't meeting your needs — but not in a critical way that could cause us to lose interest.)

Since understanding and meeting your wife's needs is the golden key to a fulfilling marriage, the rest of this book deals with that subject.

Your Wife's Needs

I believe a woman needs to be in harmony with her husband through a deep, intimate relationship. She needs comradeship, harmony, and a feeling of togetherness.

To satisfy your wife, I believe you need to make a dedicated effort to meet each of her needs explained below and expanded in later chapters.

1. Your wife needs to feel that she is very valuable in your life, more important than your mother, children, friends, sports activities, hobbies, employees, or job.

2. When your wife is stressed out and hurting, she needs to know that you are willing to share an intimate moment of comfort without demanding explanations or giving lectures.

3. She needs open or unobstructed communication.

4. She needs to be praised so she can feel a valuable part of your life.

5. She needs to feel free to help you without fearing retaliation and anger.

6. She needs to know that you will defend and protect her.

7. She needs to know that her opinion is so valuable that you will discuss decisions with her and act only after carefully evaluating her advice.

8. She needs to share her life with you in every area—home, family, and outside interests.

9. She needs you to be the kind of man her son can follow and her daughter would want to marry.

10. She needs to be tenderly held often, just to be near you, apart from times of sexual intimacy.

When her needs are met, a woman gains security and glows with a sense of well-being. Some of her glow will rub off on you, especially if you are responsible for it in the first place.

Three Safeguards

I hope you will practice these three safeguards with each chapter you read, since the ideas I put forth are general in nature.

First, discuss each chapter with your wife to see where she agrees and disagrees. Think of her as a flower. All flowers are beautiful, but each needs a specific amount of sunlight, nutrients, and water to flourish. You need to discover who she really is, especially as she changes from year to year.

Second, after she has shared her unique needs, rephrase them in your own words until *she* says you have picked up her meaning. For example, work at discovering what your wife means when she complains, "You said you'd be back in a *little while*." A little while might mean thirty minutes to her and two hours to you.

Third, it is important to remember how much you both differ as male and female. In general, a wife is naturally more sensitive and more aware of relationships than her husband. Try to understand that she will probably feel, see, and hear more than you. When your wife says something to you, allow it to sink in. Make an extra effort to understand your relationship *as she sees it*.

One Hundred Ways

The rest of this chapter is devoted to showing you one hundred ways you can love your wife *her way*. Discuss this list with your wife. Ask her to check the ones that are meaningful to her, and then arrange them in order of importance to her. Use the list as a basis for learning her views. I know your relationship will be greatly strengthened as you learn how to use these suggestions:

- ☐ Communicate with her; never close her out.
- ☐ Regard her as important.
- ☐ Do everything you can to understand her feelings.
- ☐ Be interested in her friends.
- ☐ Ask her opinion frequently.
- ☐ Value what she says.
- ☐ Let her feel your approval and affection.
- ☐ Protect her on a daily basis.
- ☐ Be gentle and tender with her.
- ☐ Develop a sense of humor.
- ☐ Avoid sudden major changes without discussion and without giving her time to adjust.
- ☐ Learn to respond openly and verbally when she wants to communicate.

☐ Comfort her when she is down emotionally. For instance, put your arms around her and silently hold her for a few seconds without lectures or put-downs.

☐ Be interested in what she feels is important in life.

☐ Correct her gently and tenderly.

☐ Allow her to teach you without putting up your defenses.

☐ Make special time available to her and your children.

☐ Be trustworthy.

☐ Compliment her often.

☐ Be creative when you express your love, either in words or actions.

☐ Have specific family goals for each year.

☐ Let her buy things she considers necessary.

☐ Be forgiving when she offends you.

☐ Show her you need her.

☐ Accept her the way she is; discover her uniqueness as special.

☐ Admit your mistakes; don't be afraid to be humble.

☐ Lead your family in their spiritual relationship with God.

☐ Allow your wife to fail; discuss what went wrong after you have comforted her.

☐ Rub her feet or neck after a hard day.

☐ Take time for the two of you to sit and talk calmly.

☐ Go on romantic outings.

☐ Write her a letter occasionally, telling her how much you love her.

☐ Surprise her with a card or flowers.

☐ Express how much you appreciate her.

☐ Tell her how proud you are of her.

- ☐ Give advice in a loving way when she asks for it.
- ☐ Defend her to others.
- ☐ Prefer her over others.
- ☐ Do not expect her to do activities beyond her emotional or physical capabilities.
- ☐ Pray for her to enjoy God's best in life.
- ☐ Take time to notice what she has done for you and the family.
- ☐ Brag about her to other people behind her back.
- ☐ Share your thoughts and feelings with her.
- ☐ Tell her about your job if she is interested.
- ☐ Take time to see how she spends her day.
- ☐ Learn to enjoy what she enjoys.
- ☐ Take care of the kids before dinner.
- ☐ Help straighten up the house before mealtime.
- ☐ Let her take a bubble bath while you do the dishes.
- ☐ Understand her physical limitations if you have several children.
- ☐ Discipline the children in love, not anger.
- ☐ Help her finish her goals—to pursue hobbies or education or career.
- ☐ Treat her as if God had stamped on her forehead, "Handle with care."
- ☐ Get rid of habits that annoy her.
- ☐ Be gentle and thoughtful to her relatives.
- ☐ Do not compare her relatives to yours in a negative way.
- ☐ Thank her for things she has done without expecting anything in return.
- ☐ Help with the housecleaning.

☐ Make sure she understands everything you are planning to do.

☐ Do little things for her — an unexpected kiss, coffee in bed.

☐ Treat her as an intellectual equal.

☐ Find out if she wants to be treated as physically weaker.

☐ Discover her fears in life.

☐ See what you can do to eliminate her fears.

☐ Discover her sexual needs.

☐ Ask if she wants to discuss how you can meet her sexual needs.

☐ Find out what makes her insecure.

☐ Plan your future together.

☐ Do not quarrel over words, but try to find hidden meanings.

☐ Practice common courtesies like holding the door for her or pouring her coffee.

☐ Ask if you offend her sexually in any way.

☐ Ask if she is jealous of anyone.

☐ See if she is uncomfortable about the way money is spent.

☐ Take her on dates now and then.

☐ Hold her hand in public.

☐ Put your arm around her in front of friends.

☐ Tell her you love her — often.

☐ Remember anniversaries, birthdays, and other special occasions.

☐ Learn to enjoy her hobbies.

☐ Teach her to hunt and fish or whatever you enjoy doing.

☐ Give her a special gift from time to time.

☐ Share the responsibilities around the house.

- ☐ Do not belittle her feminine characteristics.
- ☐ Let her express herself freely, without fear of being called stupid or illogical.
- ☐ Carefully choose your words, especially when angry.
- ☐ Do not criticize her in front of others.
- ☐ Do not let her see you become excited about the physical features of another woman.
- ☐ Be sensitive to other people.
- ☐ Let your family know you want to spend special time with them.
- ☐ Surprise her by fixing her favorite meal.
- ☐ Be sympathetic when she is sick.
- ☐ Call her when you are going to be late.
- ☐ Do not disagree with her in front of the children.
- ☐ Take her out to dinner and for weekend getaways.
- ☐ Do the "little things" she needs from time to time.
- ☐ Give her special time to be alone or with her friends.
- ☐ Buy her what she considers an intimate gift.
- ☐ Read a book she recommends to you.
- ☐ Give her a framed letter to hang on the wall, assuring her of your lasting love.
- ☐ Write her a poem about how special she is.

For Personal Reflection

1. Who did Jesus say would be the greatest in his kingdom (Matthew 20:25–28)?

2. If we desire to renew our minds and to think like Christ, we need to ask: What were his thoughts (Philippians 2:5–8)?

3. What were Paul's thoughts on the same subject (Philippians 2:17, 22, 25)?

4. If a husband is to love his wife as Christ loves the church, how does Christ love the church (Ephesians 5:25–27, 29)?

3

IF YOUR WIFE DOESN'T WIN FIRST PLACE, YOU LOSE!

■ ■ ■

"For where your treasure is,
there will your heart be also."

Matthew 6:21 KJV

I once had the opportunity to interview some of the married members of a popular cheerleading squad on an NFL football team. Although they were all obviously beautiful women, I found that they faced many of the same problems other married women do. One cheerleader said her greatest disappointment was knowing she was not the most important person in her husband's life.

"Even our dog is more important to him than I am," she said.

"He comes home and plays with the dog, and then it's more of a when's-dinner-going-to-be-ready attitude," she sighed.

A woman's sparkling affection toward her husband is diminished when he begins to prefer other activities or people over her. Many times he is not even aware of the way his misplaced priorities damage her and their relationship. For a marriage to flourish, a wife desperately needs to know she has a very special place in her husband's heart. In fact, her husband's relationship with God should be the *only* priority above his relationship with her.

Many husbands are shocked when their wives leave them "for no reason" after twenty or even thirty years of marriage. They feel they provided everything their wives could have possibly needed — a nice home, a good car, enough money to raise the children. Yet that wasn't enough. Why? A woman needs much more than things.

I have met creative businessmen who make large sums of money with their business skills and who keep their employees satisfied with respect and an awareness of their needs. Isn't it ironic that such intelligent men can go home at night and not even know how to apply the same principles to their wives? Could it be that their most important accomplishments are over at 5:00 p.m.?

Without meaning to, a husband can communicate nonverbally that other people or activities are more important to him than his wife. Haven't you heard of golf widows? Whether it is golf or tennis, church activities or community leadership, your wife and your marital happiness will suffer if most of your time and efforts are directed toward some other interest, with only cold leftovers for her. A wife can feel less important just by comparing the amount of time her husband spends with her to the time he spends elsewhere. Women notice how our eyes light up and our entire personalities change as we become excited about fishing or hunting or other activities. If your wife doesn't sense that same excitement in you when you're with her, she has a gnawing sense of failure because she feels she isn't as attractive to you as your activities or friends. This can be devastating to a woman's sense of personal worth and security.

Norma graphically illustrated this very important concept to me during our fifth year of marriage. I arrived home for lunch to find her standing quietly at the kitchen sink, not even interested in talking when I tried to make conversation. The atmosphere felt so icy that I could no longer blame the cold atmosphere on the hormonal change from a week ago. I knew I was in big trouble.

"Is there anything wrong between us?" I asked her.

"It doesn't matter. You wouldn't understand anyway," she answered.

"Funny thing, I'm losing my desire to go back to work right now. I can see there are some real problems here. Wouldn't you like to talk about it? I'm not sure what I'm doing wrong."

"Even if I told you, either you wouldn't understand or you wouldn't change, so what's the use? Let's not talk about it. It's too painful. It discourages me and disappoints me when you say you're going to do something and then you don't."

But I gently resisted, telling her that I wished she would share it with me, that I just didn't understand. Finally, she was able to verbalize what actions during the past five years had driven a wedge between us and were causing me to violate an important biblical principle.

"You'd really rather be at work, or with your friends, or counseling people than spending time with me," she said.

I asked her to explain.

"If someone calls you when we have plans, you're liable to say, 'Let me check with my wife and see if I can't postpone our plans.' I just can't believe you would do that to me over and over again."

I explained how it was easier for me to turn her down than to say no to other people.

"What about when I cook a special dinner, sometimes even with candlelight? You'll come home or call and say you've had to make other plans. You go off somewhere with other people as if I didn't even exist, as if it didn't even mean anything that I've gone to extra-special effort for you."

She continued, "I don't care anymore. I don't even want to do these special things for you. I've been disappointed so many times that I just can't handle it emotionally."

She made me realize that although I always had time for someone in need of counseling, I made little effort to spend meaningful time with her. When I did spend time with her, she said, I didn't have the same concentration or excitement about being with her.

I listened as she revealed her innermost feelings for several hours. I really didn't know what to do, and I wasn't sure I'd be able to change. But I could understand her complaints. I had neglected her and offended her with my unloving ways. However, when I agreed with her, she was unresponsive, and I could tell she was no longer expecting anything from our relationship.

She helped me discover that I was ignoring the biblical principle found in 1 Peter 3:7, and since then I've come to realize that it's the cornerstone of all relationships. *Grant her honor.* Honor basically means to attach high value, worth, or importance to a person or thing. Norma felt less important than my vocation and activities. Without realizing it, I was not honoring her as the most important person in my life, second only to my relationship with Christ.

"Could you forgive me for the way I've treated you?" I asked. "I'm willing to change. I'll really plan on changing."

"Sure, I've heard that song before," she said skeptically.

I didn't know how long it would take for me to reform. But I knew the next time someone called right before dinner I would have to ask, "Is this an emergency or can we work it out tomorrow?" I had to show her I really meant business about valuing her and meeting her needs *first.*

I *wanted* to tell her she was the most important person in my life. I really *wanted* to feel that way. At first I didn't have those feelings, but

I *wanted* to have them. As I tried to make her more important to me than anyone else, I soon began to *feel* she was top priority. Feelings *follow* thoughts and actions. In other words, the warm inner feeling I have for Norma began to burn *after* I placed the "queen's crown" upon her head. (I shouldn't have been surprised because in Matthew 6 we're told that what we treasure or value is what we'll have feelings for.)

My pride was broken, my ego bruised, and my feelings wounded in numerous falls from marital harmony during the first two years of living these principles. Because I tried so hard to make it work, Norma finally believed I was earnest in my endeavor to change. But it took *two years* to convince her — and it may take you that long to convince your wife.

I learned from Norma and other wives that women need to see effort and not hear mere promises. Give your wife time to watch you climb the mountain if she doesn't believe what you say initially. Show her you are learning to scale the cliffs and hurdle the crevices. The more *consistently* loving we are as husbands, the more trustworthy we become to our wives. Soon they will join us as we climb hand-over-hand toward the goal of a loving marriage.

The most important way I've ever expressed my love to Norma was when I finally attached a high value to her, when I decided that next to my relationship with God and his Word, she is worth more to me than anything on this earth — and she knows it.

The Evidence Wives Need Before They Will Believe Their Husbands

Wives need proof of change over a consistent period of time in at least three areas before they will believe their husbands' commitment.

Careful Listening without Justification or Argument

Can you imagine a husband being able to justify everything he ever did to hurt his wife? Wayne thought he could. He and his wife couldn't talk for more than fifteen minutes before falling into a heated argument. Inevitably, through his logical deductions, the argument ended up being her fault.

Finally, Wayne told Cathy he really wanted to change and to love her. A few hours later she suggested a quiet little vacation, just for the two of them to get reacquainted. "Couldn't we just take a week's vacation?" she asked.

"Are you kidding?" he replied, crushing her hopes for better understanding. "You mean you want us to pay rent here at the apartment and then pay for a hotel too? That's double rent!"

The topic developed into a fight that led to more fights as the months went by, until their relationship deteriorated and she finally left. He had refused to listen to her needs without arguing and lost her as a result. Tragically, even several years later, he still didn't understand what ended their relationship.

It is often difficult for a man to converse with his wife without challenging the meaning of various words she uses to explain how she feels inside. If a husband can *overlook the actual words* his wife uses to express herself and instead actively pursue *what she means*, fewer arguments will take place. Seek out the emotional nuggets that lie beneath the words. One man I know finds it almost impossible to do this. When his wife uses phrases like "You *never* do this," or "You *always* do that," he will inevitably say, "Now, dear, I don't *always* do that," or "Did I do it yesterday?" Or he begins to analyze her statement to prove its fallacy. In ten minutes, they're off on another hot discussion. It is essential in communication to look past the surface words to the real meaning behind the words. *There is no meaning in a word. Meaning is in people.*

Everyone has his or her own definition for a given word. We attach meanings to words based on our own unique experiences. So when we attempt to communicate with another person, we use words we believe will accurately convey our thoughts. For instance, in this book I may use words that you enjoy or words that irritate you. You might even be indifferent to my words because you have another frame of reference or because my definitions might be different from yours. For example, some see the word *need* and begin to think that the husband may be responsible for meeting his wife's needs, so they prefer the word *desire*. This is why I try to illustrate all the important points I make, probing for our common point of reference.

If we can stop justifying our actions and quit arguing about the words our wives use, we can get down to the heart of the matter. We can try rephrasing our wives' statements until they say we have grasped their meaning. "Is this what you're saying, dear?" or, "Is this what I'm hearing?" For years I thought that sarcasm was a spiritual gift and using it at just the right moment could defuse escalated arguments. Boy, was I wrong. At all cost, avoid sarcastic questions like, "Is this what you're having trouble saying?" A budding relationship between husband and wife can be stunted by a sarcastic tone and an attitude of male superiority.

Quickness to Admit Error

Countless wives and children have told me how their family relationships were weakened because of a husband's or father's unwillingness to admit his errors. Though husbands sometimes think admission of error reveals their weaknesses, the opposite is true. Just think back through your own life to the times when someone admitted his or her offense to you. Chances are your respect for him or her increased, not decreased.

A friend of mine told me about the time he made a racially derogatory statement to an associate during the day. The man was offended; however, the situation was not discussed. My friend drove away feeling somewhat uneasy and guilty for what he had said. Before he reached home, he turned around and drove back to confront the man.

Walking into the room, he said, "A few minutes ago I said

something very offensive to you. I know it was wrong, and I have come back to ask if you could forgive me for what I said."

The man nearly fell over. Of course he forgave him, and I'm sure his respect for my friend doubled. A humble admission of wrong produces positive results. When a husband admits he has hurt his wife, she feels better just knowing he understands, and his stock begins to rise. His admission of wrong can produce a much stronger marriage. Not only that, it demonstrates that he is a wise man because the Scriptures tell us only the wise seek correction.

Patience When She Is Reluctant to Believe You've Changed

What if you've been doing everything within your power to let your wife know she has first place in your life, and she still doesn't believe you've changed? Do you throw up your arms in disgust? Or do you gently persuade her over a period of time? I hope you choose the latter. Her initial respect for you wasn't lost overnight, and it can't be regained in a day, a week, or even a month. Show her that no matter how long it takes, you want to earn her respect. Remember, it took me two years to earn Norma's trust and regard. Just as you have to spend the rest of your life caring for your physical body through proper diet and exercise, so also will you need to spend the rest of your life nurturing and caring for your marriage in order for it to thrive.

Two Reasons Why a Wife Can Become Less Important to Her Husband

What causes a man to come home after work, pick up his young son, and kiss and cuddle him without even greeting his wife? How can a husband walk straight to the garage to begin a project without even acknowledging his arrival to his wife as he passes by her in the kitchen? Why does a man lose affection and enthusiasm for his wife after marriage? I think there are two major reasons.

First, a man will pursue and charm a woman with words or flowers or whatever he needs to do to *win* her. This is called the pursuit. He lives in a constant state of curiosity and fascination. But after the wedding, he feels he has conquered her. She is his, so he doesn't have to maintain the same level of enthusiasm and creativity as he did before they married. He begins to replace curiosity and fascination with duty and responsibility. She is his emotionally and legally. The husband may say to himself, "I have my wife. Now I need to conquer my business ... become a better hunter ... begin a family ..." Each frontier is viewed as a new conquest, a new experience.

Second, almost anything is sweet to a starving man, but when he's full, even honey nauseates him (Prov. 27:7). In a very real sense, a man is filled up when he marries because his wife is now a part of him. He believes he has experienced knowing her in every way—spiritually, emotionally, mentally, and physically. He may feel there is nothing left to know about her. As time goes on, if he's not careful, he allows duty and responsibility to trump curiosity and fascination. Routine trumps fun, play, and laughter, and he may be tempted to look for adventure outside of the marriage rather than rediscovering "frontiers" in his own home.

For this reason, guys, you must look for ways to inject adventure into your marriage. Early in your marriage you lived in curiosity and fascination. When you learned something new about your wife, you had plenty of "ah-ha" moments that left you wanting more. To regain that feeling, learn to ask great questions again, like, "If you could try out any occupation for a year, what would it be?" or, "How would you describe me to a stranger?" or, "Name one thing you miss about our dating relationship." Also, find ways to introduce fresh experiences into your marriage, perhaps through travel, trying a new sport, or tackling a home project together. As you encounter new challenges and experiences, you will learn new aspects of your wife's character and grow to appreciate her more.

How to Gain Your Wife's Love and More

If it came down to an evening with your friends or a night with your wife, she needs to know you would choose her company just because you enjoy being with her. In the same way, if it came to the children or her, she needs to know she would be your choice. She needs to know she's number one. When she is satisfied that she's in first place in your life, she will encourage you to do the other things you like doing. For example, when I first wrote this book over thirty years ago, I took six weeks away from my wife and children. As a young bride, Norma would have been crushed at the mere suggestion of such a long separation. Yet during the writing process she was as enthusiastic about it as I was because she knew I would be able to fulfill our dream of writing our inner convictions about marriage. More importantly, she knew I would rather be with her than with my ghost writers and editors.

One more example, but forty-five years later: For years Norma put up with my ten thousand new ideas of how to help couples. Most of those ideas never became reality, but she was always faithful to listen, give her opinions, and watch me fail time and time again. She supported me during my national TV years and through fifty-eight books and countless video tapings. Now she is taking over the reins of our marriage and family company, the Smalley Relationship Center. She manages the staff, books my speaking schedule, sells our products at our seminars, makes sure that our website is operating effectively, and helps to coordinate my writing projects. I'm becoming her number one fan just like she has been mine for all of these years.

Putting your wife in the number one slot just below God doesn't shackle you to the house; instead, it frees you of the dread of going home.

"Why don't you let me go to the meeting alone tonight so you can go to the basketball game?" Mary asked. Her husband was pleasantly shocked. Not so long ago they had had misunderstandings about his insatiable appetite for basketball. In fact, they were thinking about separating because he did not have the knowledge or skills he needed to treat Mary right, and she did not have the emotional strength to continue living with him or loving him. Today he regularly puts her before his work and other activities. And Mary is now free to encourage his outside interests, knowing she's at the top of his list.

My wife also encourages me to enjoy my interests in hunting and fishing because she feels secure in her position of importance. If an emergency arose, she knows my first commitment would be taking care of her or the children, not tending to my recreational enjoyment.

The more important a woman feels she is to her husband, the more she encourages him to do the activities she knows he enjoys.

Do you wonder whether your wife feels she is more important to you than other people or things in your life? Complete the following exercise, and I think you will find out.

1. List your favorite spare-time activities.

_____

_____

_____

2. What non-work activities do you typically engage in during the week? Include volunteer, church, house, and family commitments, as well as any leisure activities.

Monday _____

Tuesday _____

Wednesday _____

Thursday _____

Friday _____

Saturday _____

Sunday _____

3. Where do you enjoy taking your vacations? If you don't take
   vacations, is there something else you choose in place of vacation time?

   _____

   _____

   _____

Now, look back over these three lists and ask yourself, "Is there
anything on the lists I would rather do than be with my wife?" Probably so. And if so, chances are you have already communicated to
your wife that she is not as important to you as your activities, even
though you have never uttered those words. Since a woman has tremendous perception, she knows where your heart is, even when you
haven't said a word. But that doesn't mean it's too late to adjust your
priorities.

Your Wife's "Radar" Can Detect Your Sincerity

What a man values, he takes good care of. Or as Christ said, "Where
your treasure is, there will your heart be also" (Matt. 6:21 KJV).
If your hobby is fishing, you probably hesitate to loan out your
best rod and reel. If you enjoy volunteering at church, you probably spend hours there each week. Based on the amount of time or
effort you spend on each activity, your wife can sense which is most
important to you. If she doesn't feel that you are as careful with
her as you are with your other interests, she will know she is not
as important. That feeling shatters her self-worth and can result in
physical as well as emotional problems. The emotions she struggles
with now may surface years later in the form of serious and expensive
physical problems.

However, some husbands feel threatened by the thought of giving their wives special treatment, fearing they will lose out with their friends, career, or hobbies. They falsely believe if they give up other activities for the sake of being with their wives, they will give them up forever. Remember, when a wife feels she is the most important, she gets excited about her husband being able to do the things he wants to do. But don't try and deceive her! Simply telling her she's first so she'll let you out to do what you want doesn't work. In fact, if she finds out you've tried to manipulate her, you may be faced with major problems concerning her trust in you and her own feelings of worth.

How I Gained My Wife's Love and Everything Else

After ten years of marriage, I felt I was finally becoming a success at my work. I was privileged to speak regularly for various organizations in our city and throughout the country. My wife and I had a beautiful home and two children. What more could a man want? Then from my point of view, a tragedy occurred in my marriage. Norma became pregnant with our third child. I was not enthusiastic. If anything, I was depressed, realizing our youngest had only been out of diapers for two years. I was just starting to enjoy my children, and the thought of another little baby around the house was almost overwhelming, particularly when the doctor had told us specifically that we couldn't have any more children.

Although I tried to be nice to Norma, I couldn't hide my disappointment. I was afraid I might not be able to travel as much and would be forced to take a less prestigious position in the company. My work load increased as the months passed, and I warned my wife I would not be able to help her with the children because of job demands. Even on the day our son Michael was born, I worried about the added hardships he would add to my vocational dreams.

Norma's health suffered during the first year after Michael's birth because of the long night hours and the responsibility of taking care of two other small children. Michael had to have surgery and was often sick, adding to her burden. How insensitive I was during that year! Whenever the baby would cry at night or need special attention, I would quickly remind Norma he was her child. She had wanted another baby, not I.

A year passed in this way before Norma finally said to me, "I can't take it anymore. I wish I had the emotional and physical strength to take care of the kids and discipline and train them, but I just can't do it with an absentee father."

She wasn't demanding. She wasn't angry. She was simply stating the facts. She had had it. I could see the *urgency* and *calmness* in her facial expressions and realized that she desperately needed my help. I faced a major decision. Should I go to my boss and ask for a different job in the company, one that would allow me more time at home? It was a struggle because I knew I could get a less prestigious and less lucrative job, but I would have to sacrifice some of my career goals. Inwardly, I felt resentment toward my son and my wife for being weak. But I gave in. In nervousness and embarrassment, I approached my boss to explain I needed more time at home because of the children. "Is there any possibility that I could have a different job that would allow me to stay home more?"

My boss graciously cooperated by giving me another job. But to me the new job was a demotion. I was asked to do some things that only a few weeks earlier I had been training my subordinates to do. What a blow, which did nothing but fuel my resentment.

I was devastated for a while, but soon I became interested in home life. I actually looked forward to five o'clock. My family and I began doing more things together, like camping and other special activities. Before long, a deeper love blossomed within both Norma and me. Norma began to feel more physically alert, which, in turn, made her more cheerful and outgoing. She changed some habits

I disliked without any pressure from me. My big career sacrifice seemed smaller every day in comparison to the richer relationship we were developing.

Within a few months, my boss gave me a new position in the company that I liked much better than the one I had given up. By this time, Norma was so secure with me that she had no resentment toward my new job or any necessary travel that went with it. I gave in and gave up at first, but I won in the long run. That's almost exactly how Christ explains the principle of exchange in Mark 8:35: "For whoever wants to save their life will lose it, but whoever loses their life for me and for the gospel will save it" (NIV).

God not only used Michael to bring me back to the family and center my priorities, but he gave me Michael to save my life. In 2004 Michael gave me one of his kidneys. While I might have thought I was sacrificing my life for him when he was a baby, he is the one who sacrificed for me. I am truly humbled by his gift.

The Incredible Results of Making Your Wife Feel Important

One morning Sandy was so sexually responsive to Rick that he was stunned and surprised by her excitement. How did Rick motivate her? With one very simple statement. He was getting ready for work that morning, running a little late, when he heard Sandy complaining of a growing headache and neck ache.

"Let me rub your neck," he offered.

"No, you don't have time," she replied. "You've got to get to work."

His usual response would have been, "Yeah, you're right. I don't want to be late. But I hope you feel better. Take an aspirin."

On this particular morning he said, "I tell you what. I'd rather be with you any day. Let me rub your neck." As he gently massaged her tense muscles, he continued, "Work can wait ... you're more important to me." She was so thrilled with his attitude and so encouraged by his sensitivity and gentleness that she said she could hardly resist giving herself to him in every way.

We men are often not aware of the effect we have on our wives by being gentle and tender, showing our unshakable devotion. Do you want a more enjoyable marriage? It's possible. And it all starts by loving your wife more than any person or any activity.

Here are a few questions you can ask your wife to open up a discussion concerning her real feelings about the place she shares in your life:

1. Do you feel you are the most important person in my life?
2. Are there any activities in my life you feel are more important to me than you are?
3. Are there any special ways you believe I could better communicate how important you are to me?

Remember, the more you do to build a valuable, healthy relationship, the better you'll feel about your marriage. If you change any of your activities because you want to enrich your relationship, at first you may feel you're giving up your favorite pastime. But in the long run, you'll not only gain a better marriage, but a greater freedom to enjoy other areas of life. Today I wouldn't trade my deep friendship with Norma for anything on this earth. I am finding that the more important a man's wife is to him, the more she encourages him to enjoy life.

For Personal Reflection

1. What is the basic meaning of the word *honor*? See 1 Peter 3:7.
2. How can your emotional feelings for your mate grow? See Matthew 6:21.

4

YOUR WIFE NEEDS YOUR SHOULDER, NOT YOUR MOUTH

■ ■ ■

Put on a heart of compassion, kindness, humility,
gentleness and patience.
Colossians 3:12

As I pulled into the driveway, I heard a sickening thump under the tire. Only a few seconds earlier our cat had been running expectantly toward our car to welcome us home.

"Watch out for Puff," Norma had said.

"Oh, he'll get out of the way," I'd replied.

I hadn't been driving fast. *How fast can you pull into a driveway?* I thought.

"Oh, no!" I whispered. "Can someone get me out of this mess?"

My family thought it was just another one of my jokes about wanting to get rid of our two cats.

Our oldest son jumped out of the car, looked underneath, and fell to the ground screaming. Our daughter began sobbing, and our youngest son woke up from his nap to join the chorus. Bedlam set in. They all started accusing me of purposely killing the cat. In fact, I was accused of things that would have put me in jail for years. How I regretted the times I had joked about getting rid of the cats.

Puff was the kitten of our other cat. We all loved the mother cat, but they loved Puff much more. We had kept the kitten because of his "puffy" hernia. His stomach grew larger and larger until finally I had to give in and take him to a veterinarian to have the hernia repaired. But the operation was a failure. A few months later I had to take him back for another operation. And I didn't even want the cat in the first place. I told my family, "This cat sure is costing me a lot." I was saying things some men typically say, blind to the hurt I was causing my family.

Now that I had run over the cat, I was under attack. When they started screaming at me, I wanted to yell back. But the things Norma had shared with me in the past about herself and our children strangled the words. "Don't talk. Just hold me or hold the kids whenever there's a tragedy," she had said.

They were making so much racket in the front yard that I knew the neighbors were going to think I was killing them. I was so embarrassed and crushed that I herded them all into the house. Then I put my arm around Kari and hugged her. But as I hugged Greg, I could tell he didn't want me to touch him. I tried to put my arm around Norma, but she gave me one of those looks a woman saves for times when her husband bombs out.

"This is what you always wanted, isn't it?" she asked. "You wanted him dead." With that, she marched into the bedroom and closed the door.

But I still didn't say anything. I didn't get angry, although I felt my family misunderstood me. I knew that raising my voice wouldn't help. Since Michael didn't want me to touch him either, Greg and I went out to the driveway to get Puff and bury him. We took him to our little burial ground where Peter, our rabbit, rests. Greg was still sobbing, "Dad, life will never be the same." Greg loved that cat just about as much as you can love anything. As Greg and I buried him, I prayed, and Greg concluded the funeral service.

I felt nauseous as I went back inside. There stood twelve-year-old Kari comforting five-year-old Michael. "Michael, it was Puff's time to go. It was Puff's time," she said.

When Greg was getting ready for bed, I went to his room and held him. His eyes red, he asked, "Dad, what am I going to do when I come home from school? Puff won't be there to jump into my arms." And like Greg, I had tears streaming down my cheeks.

Courageous little Kari was standing in the hall after putting Michael to bed. "Well, Dad, it's all over," she said. "It was Puff's time. I tell you what, Dad, I think we can eat those donuts now." (We had bought donuts and milk after church, planning a quiet family snack.)

"Kari, you can if you want, but I just wouldn't be able to eat. I just can't eat tonight," I told her.

Opening the door to our bedroom, I wondered if my wife was ready to face me yet. She had told me many times in the past, "Don't demand anything. Wait until I am able to respond to you."

I got down on my knees next to her, gently touched her hand, and asked, "How are you feeling?"

"I'm feeling better. I know you didn't mean to murder Puff," she said.

I could have reacted to her statement in anger, but I only said, "That's okay. I understand. You know all those things I said when I was joking about Puff? I really feel bad about them. You can rest assured I'll never joke about things like that again. Would it make you feel better if we made Angel an inside cat from now on?"

From time to time for a few weeks, I would say to Norma, "You know, I really do feel bad that you don't have Puff around to jump up into your arms." She would put her head down on my shoulder and say, "Yeah, I know, I feel bad too." Through that painful experience, I learned more about comforting my wife than I could have in years of trouble-free existence.

Meeting Your Wife's Needs

Who is best equipped to teach you how to meet your wife's needs? Hint: It's not me. And it's not you. It's your wife. Let *her* teach you how you can best meet her needs during a crisis or when she's discouraged and losing energy.

Probably the most important lesson my wife taught me on how to comfort her was when she told me in a calm way that she could not handle my busy work schedule along with the pressures of the children and the home. By coming to me without threats to explain her limitations, she touched something within me. I was eager to comfort her. I don't know if she stirred my protective manly feelings or what, but when she told me she couldn't take the pressure I was putting on her and that she might be close to a collapse, I was motivated to relieve her of that pressure.

I have found that this nonthreatening approach works even in a father-daughter relationship. A university graduate student came to me because of a poor relationship with her father. Financially, he had been very generous to her, but she needed his love and gentleness much more than she needed his money. I tried to work with her father, explaining what I had learned about women. "Comfort her," I suggested. "Be tender and gentle. Don't lecture her." He couldn't grasp it, although he is a very skillful and intelligent lawyer, quite successful in his profession.

"I tried to take my life last week," this young woman told me. "I just cannot handle the emotional pressure I'm under with my father."

"You've got choices," I said.

"What?"

"You can respond to your father in a way that you and I know will bring healing to your life."

"I'm not able to do that," she said wearily.

"Okay, then you can call your father and say to him, 'Daddy, I love you. I wish that I could spend more time with you, but, Daddy, I feel like I just can't handle seeing you right now. I can't emotionally handle the way you treat me—your lectures, your insensitivity, and your harshness. As much as I wish I could, as much as I wish I were stronger, I just can't handle it right now.'"

This young woman has unique needs and qualities. Nobody could tell her she needed to be stronger. She is who she is. To tell her to be what she can't be is like saying to the sun, "Don't come up tomorrow." It's not reality!

Happily, her father was motivated to change, thinking, "I must really be insensitive. My own daughter can't handle my presence. She can't even handle a phone call from me."

Many men don't realize that tender love through a gentle touch and listening ear is all a woman needs at times—just a comforting hug, a loving statement like, "I understand. You're hurting, aren't you? You're feeling under a lot of pressure, aren't you?" Listening to her talk without making critical comments or offering quick solutions is important.

Give Her Your Shoulder, Not Your Mouth

One of the greatest truths that I continue to learn each day is that I don't have what it takes to be a genuinely loving husband or father. I believe that most husbands are as incapable of loving in a real and lasting way as I am. So, one of my main habits I've been developing for many years is to admit that I'm helpless when it comes to loving others. As a human, I just don't possess the ability to do this great act on my own. Christ told us over two thousand years ago that God only gives his love and power to those who admit that they are "beggars" when it comes to the "spiritual kind of love." This is the kind of love that gives a man the ability to love his wife in ways that reflect patience, kindness, selflessness, and all of the other great qualities of love found in 1 Corinthians 13. Men, I am still finding the power from God to love my wife as I remain aware of my helplessness to do it on my own. I'm like a newborn child; I can't feed myself love without God.

As you rely on God's love, make it your goal to become a gentle, loving, and tender husband who does not lecture. Lectures during stressful times only create more stress. As a young husband this was a new concept to me, because I wasn't fortunate enough to have a father who knew how to be tender to his wife, and I wasn't initially aware of my wife's need for tenderness. No one had ever told me that one of a woman's greatest needs is tenderness and a husband who will listen instead of lecture, and even if someone had, I don't think I would have understood. (I should have been able to figure it out, though, because when I am down, I like people to be gentle and comforting to me.)

I'll never forget what one woman told me: "I wish my husband would put his arms around me and hold me, without lecturing me, when I am feeling blue." But lecture number 734 would begin as he told her she would feel better if she took an aspirin ... if she were more organized ... if she wouldn't wear herself down so much ... if she would discipline the children better....

"Have you ever told him what you need?" I asked.

"Are you kidding? I'd be embarrassed," she laughed.

"He probably doesn't know what to do," I told her. "He doesn't know you need to be held instead of lectured. Why don't you tell him during a calm conversation some day?"

"That does kind of make sense to me. A lot of times when I am down and crying and all upset, he'll ask, 'What do you want me to do?' I just flare up and say, 'If I have to tell you what to do, it would wreck the whole idea.' "

Your wife might long for you to be a mind reader, but I think common sense will compel her to settle for this: a husband who calmly and gently asks her what she needs, listens to her answer, then responds by filling that need. What could be better?

Practice, Practice, Practice

As a husband, I recommend that you ask your wife when and how you need to hold her when she needs to be comforted. Ask her what circumstances prompt her to seek your gentle caring arms and touch. You can't dream them up on your own. We just can't perceive the deep feelings of other people. We've got to draw them out and then *practice, practice, practice* the skills of meeting our wives' needs.

The first time I ever tried to ski, I rode a rope pulley to the top of a small hill. The hill looked a lot bigger from the top than it did from the bottom.

I thought, "No way am I gonna go down this hill." So I sat down on the back of my skis and scooted all the way down.

Even if you have to scoot instead of ski your way through the skills in this chapter at first, remember that you'll eventually be able to get to your feet. This book is certainly not an exhaustive marriage manual, but it is a start. Believe me, if you practice what is written here, you and your wife can have a more loving marriage.

When I was first learning the art of comforting my wife, we had an experience that took every ounce of self-control I could muster. But I came through a stronger man, encouraged by my new-found strength. I want you to imagine yourself in my situation. How would you have reacted?

I had bought a dumpy-looking boat for four hundred dollars because we wanted to do more things together as a family. That same night, my son and I decided to take it for a quick trip to the lake only five minutes from our house, just to see how it ran. Because of my inexperience as a boater, the wind blew the boat back to the bank the first time I put it in. I got wet and frustrated trying to push it out again. After we spent an irritating ten minutes trying to start the cantankerous thing, the boat wouldn't go faster than ten miles an hour. Something was obviously wrong. I was quite a way from the shore before I realized I had better get back in case the motor stalled.

Then—"Dad, the boat's sinking!" Greg cried. I looked behind me and saw the foot of water that had gurgled in. The previous owner had taken the plug out the last time it had rained but had forgotten to tell me. With the hull full of water, I couldn't find the hole for the plug. Luckily we didn't sink. I put the boat back on the trailer, determined to take it back first thing in the morning. A boat dealer told me it would take one hundred and fifty dollars to fix the engine's broken seal, so I returned it to the owner, who had promised me I could have my money back if I didn't like it.

When I left home early that morning, I had agreed to be back by eleven o'clock so Norma could go shopping. Retrieving my money took longer than I had planned, and I arrived home an hour-and-a-half late. In the meantime, Norma had decided to take our mini motor home to the grocery store. Trying to turn it around in the driveway, she accidentally drove too close to the house and sheared off a section of the roof. As the roof fell, it put a huge dent in the front of the motor home.

When I pulled into the driveway at half past noon, I saw part of the roof lying in the driveway next to the dented motor home. I was overcome by emotion. I had no clue what to say or do as I approached Norma.

I wanted to yell, "It will cost at least five hundred dollars to fix this! Where did you get your driver's license, at a garage sale?" I wanted to lecture Norma angrily and then ignore her for a while. Instead I nervously repeated in what I thought was a quiet voice, "What should I do? What should I do?"

My son Greg overheard me. "Dad, why don't you do what you teach?" he reminded me.

Smart aleck, I thought. But then I quickly asked, "What do I teach?"

He said, "You teach that mom is way more important than things."

Thanks to Greg, I remembered what I was supposed to do. I told myself, "Keep your mouth shut and put your arms around her. Just hold her. Don't say anything, okay?"

Everything in me screamed, "Let your anger out! Express it!" But I put my arms around Norma and said gently, "You must feel terrible, don't you?" We went into the house and sat on the couch, and I let her talk her feelings out.

I held her, and after a couple of minutes I felt good because I could feel the tenderness begin to flow from me. Soon I was fine, and she was encouraged. Minutes later, a carpenter friend who had already heard about the accident drove up. We had the roof patched and painted in two hours.

It felt good not to be angry for once. I hadn't offended my wife, shouted at the kids, or diminished any of the beauty of our relationship. I could have reverted to my old excuse, "Well, I just can't keep from blowing up." Instead, I had an encouraging victory.

My newfound sensitivity was tested on several occasions. Once I almost blew it on a fishing trip. I normally become completely oblivious to my family and the world when I'm near a stream, totally submerging myself in the exhilarating environment of fishing: the smell of the air, the tension when a fish strikes, the sound of the stream.... Oops! Back to the story.

When we pulled our mini motor home beside a beautiful stream, my heart was pounding. I could hardly wait to get my reel rigged up. First, I rigged the kids' reels and told them, "Look, if you get tangled up, you're on your own." (I used to get so frustrated when I was trying to fish and they were yelling, "Dad, I can't get this reeled in." I wanted to devote my entire energy to fishing on my own.)

I found the perfect spot: a nice deep hole in a pool in front of a big boulder. I threw in the lure and let it wander naturally to the bottom of the pool. It swirled around and WHAM! I got my first trout. I had nearly caught the limit when Greg came running up. I was sure he was about to jump into the stream and spook the fish. I was already upset and angry from his interruption when he said, "Dad! Kari broke her leg!"

Kari broke her leg? What a time to break her leg! I couldn't believe she would do this to me. It was hard for me to leave, but I gave the line to Greg and said, "Don't break it. Don't get it tangled up. Just keep it in there." I ran in Kari's direction, avoiding the big pool. After all, I didn't want to scare the fish.

Downstream, Kari was crying. "Daddy, I think I broke my leg."

When I looked at it, I realized it was only bruised from a bad fall. "Why didn't you look first?" I lectured her. "You know rocks are slippery when they're wet. Now don't touch it. It's not broken, it's just bruised. Put your leg in this cold water to soak for a few minutes."

I'm really embarrassed to tell the rest of the story, but maybe you can learn from my insensitivity. I ran back to the fishing hole and caught a few more trout before walking back to where Kari was crying. "Dad, this water is cold."

I rather roughly got her up to walk, but she couldn't. When I tried to hoist her up on the bank and couldn't, she started crying again and said, "Dad, you're so rough with me. Can't you be *tender*?"

Something flashed when she said that word. It reminded me of all the times my wife and other women have told me, "What we need is tenderness and gentleness, not harshness. We don't need lectures." And I couldn't even be tender with my eleven-year-old daughter. Just what was more important anyway? Those trout or my precious daughter? It was hard for me to face it, but those trout had been more important to me. I had let fishing and my own desires endanger my only daughter. I was wrong, and I should have known better.

When I came to my senses, I hung my head low and said, "Kari, I've been so wrong to be harsh with you. I really feel bad. Would you forgive me?"

"Yeah, I'll forgive you, Dad."

"Kari, you are more important to me than any fish, and I want you to know that. I was so carried away by this activity today that I really hurt you, didn't I?"

We just held each other for a while, and then she looked up into my eyes and asked gently, "Dad, did you use deodorant today?"

Helping Your Wife Overcome Depression

Both men and women experience stress daily. Psychologists tell us that stressful experiences and prolonged anger affect our minds, our emotions, and our bodies. The amount of stress we experience in each of these areas can mean the difference between happiness or depression. Positive input in any *one* area has been proven to have beneficial effects on all the other areas. If a husband is tender with his wife, for example, he lifts her emotions and, in turn, helps her in other dimensions of her life.

As a husband, you need to know the signs of depression in order to be able to comfort your wife more effectively. According to the *DSM-IV*, a manual used to diagnose mental disorders, depression occurs when someone has at least five of the following nine symptoms at the same time:

- a depressed mood during most of the day, particularly in the morning
- fatigue or loss of energy almost every day
- feelings of worthlessness or guilt almost every day
- impaired concentration, indecisiveness
- insomnia or hypersomnia (excessive sleeping) almost every day
- markedly diminished interest or pleasure in almost all activities nearly every day
- recurring thoughts of death or suicide (not just fearing death)

- a sense of restlessness — known as psychomotor agitation — or being slowed down — retardation
- significant weight loss or gain (a change of more than 5 percent of body weight in a month)

Should you detect these symptoms in your wife, you should comfort her first with statements like, "Honey, I'm not sure I know how you feel, but I really want to. And I want to help you work through whatever it is that is discouraging you." Then use the information below as a guideline to *help her* out of depression. Remember, if your wife is depressed, it may or may not be something you've contributed to — but it is *always* your responsibility to help.

1. If your wife has at least five of the above symptoms, encourage her to have a complete physical examination. Her symptoms might be caused by a hormone or vitamin deficiency or by a physical or mental illness. Most doctors are also equipped to prescribe antidepressants, which will give her brain the chemical boost needed to begin the climb out of depression.

2. Avoid lecturing her. Arguing with her only makes her feel you don't understand. But sending her a card or flowers can lift her emotionally. Help your children do something special for her. For example, you can go down to the store and buy a small roll of shelf paper. Roll it out and on it paste magazine pictures that depict things you appreciate about her. With brightly colored pens, write affectionate words all over the banner. Roll it up with a pretty bow and present it to her as a family. Your thoughtful gesture will affect her emotions and help lift her out of the darkness.

3. Listen to your wife with the "third ear." In other words, listen for her emotional message. What is she trying to say? Can you understand the meaning behind her words? Try saying something like, "I don't know why this terrible thing has happened

to you, but I can really see that it has deeply upset you." By saying those words, you will allow her time to gain physical strength through your understanding.

4. Another helpful therapy for depression is journaling. Buy your wife a notebook and encourage her to write down her feelings and the ways you or others have hurt her. Better yet, encourage her to write down the benefits that will enter her life as a result of the depressing things that have happened to her. She may resist at first, saying she can't think of a single benefit. You may need to come up with at least one benefit for her before she can get started. The more benefits she uncovers, the better she will feel. Most women who do this exercise end up telling me, "Things really aren't so bad." In fact, this is so important that I've written an entire book to help people find value in troubled times. *Joy That Lasts* can assist you in helping your wife actually find benefit in trials and gain a whole new perspective on anger, worry, fear, hurt feelings, and guilt.

   Even when your wife can't take time to write down her feelings, you can help her avoid negative thinking. Gently steer her away from the two words, "If only." Those two words have kept more people in depression than any others. "If only I hadn't ... if only I would ... if only he had ..." Those two words can tear up a person emotionally, mentally, and physically.

5. During stressful times, encourage your wife to relax her muscles. I practice regularly an exercise recommended by Dr. Jerry Day, a clinical psychologist. I can personally testify that this ten-minute relaxation technique has, at times, made me feel like I've just had four hours of deep sleep. It renews creativity and strength.

   Relax in a chair or on a bed. Take several deep breaths, then tighten every muscle in your body for as long as you can hold in one deep breath, and then exhale. Visualize your muscles relaxing, and then don't move a muscle for the remainder of the ten minutes.

6. Help your wife begin and continue a vigorous physical exercise program. Norma takes walks daily, even at seventy years of age. Physical exercise helps a person mentally and emotionally. Those who work with depressed people say exercise is one of the most important areas of therapy, and in some cases exercise has been found to be as effective as antidepressants. So give your wife the time and place where she can get the exercise she needs and enjoys. If that means investing in a membership to a health club or equipment for your home or getting a babysitter so she can run, spend the money, knowing an ounce of prevention is worth a pound of cure.

7. Part of being wise is discerning when we need help as well. If your wife gets and stays depressed for longer than three weeks and is not helped by exercise or antidepressants, you need to think seriously about calling a Christian counselor or psychiatrist to help address your wife's illness.

A Healing Balm on a Hurting Soul

A military officer once told me his story of how he loved his wife back to emotional health. For years she had suffered from severe depression, and the psychiatrist had recommended that his wife be admitted to the local mental hospital. The officer, dismayed at the news, sought counsel from his chaplain. After hearing his story, the chaplain advised the officer to have his wife sit in his lap and share her true feelings about him.

The officer followed this advice with great difficulty because it hurt to hear the things she said he was doing to weaken their marriage. As she was talking, the telephone rang, and he felt "saved by the bell." She was angry because she thought he would probably not

YOUR WIFE NEEDS YOUR SHOULDER, NOT YOUR MOUTH

return. But she overheard something that not only kept her from a breakdown but prompted her to slip into a nightgown and actually desire to arouse him (something she had not done in years). After the call, she calmly snuggled back into his lap.

What had he said to his commanding officer?

He simply said, "Sir, could someone else take that assignment tonight? I'm in the middle of a very important time with my wife. It's serious, and I really don't want to leave at this point." That military officer had begun to prove to his wife that she was of high value to him. As a result, her mental condition stabilized, and she never had to go to the hospital. While love cannot cure all ills and some problems require medication or further counseling, a husband's tender love can certainly act as a healing balm on a hurting soul.

For Personal Reflection

1. Is it natural to be comforting and gentle during tension or a crisis? See Colossians 3:8–14; 4:6.

2. Do you understand your wife's needs during a crisis? See 1 Peter 3:7. Write out her response to this question too.

5

CLIMBING OUT OF
MARRIAGE'S DEEPEST PIT

■ ■ ■

*"It is inevitable that stumbling blocks should come, but
woe to him through whom they come!"*

Luke 17:1

It was 4:00 p.m. on Valentine's Day when I remembered my basketball game. I reached for the phone to call Norma, my bride of less than a year. "Honey, I forgot to tell you I have a basketball game tonight. We're supposed to be there about 7:00 p.m. I'll pick you up about 6:30."

Silence hung heavily on the line before she answered, "But this is Valentine's Day."

"Yeah, I know, but I need to be there tonight because I promised the team. I don't want to let them down."

"But I have a special dinner prepared with candles and—"

"Can you hold it off until tomorrow?" She didn't answer, so I continued. (What I was about to say caused a great deal of damage in our relationship. Like many young husbands, I didn't have the slightest hint of how deeply this would wound her.) "Honey, you know how important it is for a wife to submit to her husband. I really need to be there tonight, and if we're going to start off with good habits in the early part of our marriage, now is the time to begin. If I'm going to be the leader of this family, I need to make the decision."

"Ice" perfectly describes the reception I received when I picked her up. It was easy to see I had severely offended her, but I figured she had to learn to be submissive sometime, and we might as well start now.

The lifeless expression on her face grew worse as the evening wore on. When we returned home after the game, I noticed that the table was all set up for a special dinner—candles, our best dishes, and pretty napkins. Balloons sagging over the coffee table. She still wasn't speaking to me the next day, so I rushed to the florist to gather a variety of flowers, which I put in various spots all over the house. That warmed her up a little. Then I gave her a giant card with a hand on the front that could be turned thumbs up or thumbs down. "Which way is it?" I asked her. She turned it thumbs up. I never said whether I was right or wrong, only that I felt badly about the night before. And so began a history of offenses I never knew how to clear up with her.

Had someone not shared with me later the secret of developing a lasting and intimate relationship, we might have joined the millions who seek divorce each year.

Couples often ask me, "Where have we gone wrong?" "Why don't we feel romantic toward each other?" "How come we argue so much?" "Why do we avoid touching each other?" These problems are not primarily attributable to incompatibility, sexual problems, financial pressure, or any other surface issues. They are a direct result of accumulated offenses that cause anger to grow within each other. If a husband and wife can understand how to maintain harmony by immediately working to clear up every hurtful offense between them, they can climb out of such common problems and even marriage's deepest pit — divorce. As much as possible, you need to end every day with a clean slate — no offenses between the two of you.

How Did I Get Down Here Anyway?

When a man treats his wife carelessly, she is usually offended far deeper than he realizes. She begins to close him out, and if he continues to hurt her feelings, she will separate herself from him mentally, emotionally, and physically. In other words, she doesn't want any contact in any way with him. Haven't you noticed how your wife clams up after you have insulted her? She not only avoids conversation, but also avoids being touched. *A wife simply will not respond to her husband when he continually hurts her feelings without "clearing the slate" — draining away her anger.* In forty-five years of marriage, I can't begin to tell you the number of times my wife's spirit has closed toward me. It usually came as the result of me trying to change her. If I noticed behaviors in her that I didn't like or I thought she didn't notice, I would bring them to her attention. Even with good intentions, I shut her down and she closed her heart to me time and again.

Some people justify their reactions by saying, "But he/she hurt my feelings." There's no such thing as hurt feelings, according to psychologist Dr. Henry Brandt. He says, "Let's call hurt feelings what they really are — anger." It isn't right for your wife to react in anger, but that's not the point of this book. Our goal as husbands should be to guard our hearts and words and adjust our behavior so our wives don't shut down and react in anger.

To understand why your wife naturally clams up when you offend her, think about how this principle applies to a job. Did you ever quit because you weren't happy with the boss or working conditions? I remember how much I loved one job until the boss offended me deeply. At that moment, my mind became tangled in a web of reasons to leave. Although I knew what was going on inside me, I couldn't seem to control my emotions. They had changed, and I wasn't as fond of the work as I had been. I eventually didn't want to show up or have anything to do with that job.

We tend to follow a natural pattern when we've been offended. Mentally, we are more alert to the flaws of the offender. Emotionally, we feel estranged. Physically, we avoid that person. And spiritually, we close out the person (Prov. 15:13).

I have watched my wife go through this process many times. When I played basketball that Valentine's evening instead of going home to her romantic candlelit dinner, she was so hurt and disappointed that she didn't want to talk to me. She didn't want to touch me or have me touch her.

Have you ever put your arm around your wife after provoking her and felt her tighten up? You may not know that you have criticized her when that happened. But you need to accept the responsibility for her coldness and say, "I want to understand how you feel, and I don't blame you for not wanting me near you right now. I'm very sure that what I did is so obvious to you, but I'm so thickheaded, I missed it." After you understand, then you can ask for her forgiveness. She is much more willing to forgive you after you greatly increase your understanding of the situation.

If your wife does not want you to touch her, if she has lost some of that romantic "spark" she once had for you, or if she is plotting ways to get away from you even for short periods of time, you can be sure you have offended her and possibly "closed" her spirit. (If you need even more explanation about how anger affects others, my book *The Key to Your Child's Heart* explains in detail about what "closes" a person's spirit and specific ways in which we can "reopen" it.)

A not-so-funny thing happened on the way to a party one evening. Norma teasingly said she planned to play a joke on the company president, a joke that would have embarrassed me. I couldn't believe she would consider such a thing, and I said, "Norma, you can't do that. I'm not going tonight if you really plan on doing it."

She kidded around with me a little more, and I stopped the car and with harshness and impatience yelled, "I'm not going! I would be too embarrassed to go there."

Norma admitted she really wasn't serious, but my persistent harshness was too much for her (Prov. 15:4). Because I was so abusive, she began to cry. Realizing I had done the wrong thing, I tried to make it right. The more I talked, the worse it grew. At the party, whenever I glanced at her, she looked away. She was thinking of all the reasons her husband wasn't such a "great catch" anymore. It took days for me to reestablish harmony.

What does a man have to do to clear up offenses against his wife? How can he maintain harmony with her?

Maintaining Harmony

Harmony can be defined as the absence of unsettled offenses between the two of you. When a real harmony and oneness exist between you and your wife, the two of you will want to relax and spend time talking. Your wife will be more agreeable. She will feel emotionally and physically attracted to you. But when you have offended her, she will probably *resist* you and *argue* with you. If she is reacting to you and saying things like, "No, it's red, I saw it," and you say, "No, it was blue," don't be surprised if she didn't see the real color because anger can cause "color blindness." And the same goes for you. You both may see different colors depending upon the level of unresolved anger in your hearts.

Wives are often accused of being strong-willed and rebellious when, in reality, they're simply responding to their husbands' thoughtless abuses. They are sometimes accused of wrecking marriages because they have lost affectionate or romantic love for their husbands. Of course, husbands seldom realize that their insensitive behavior is what ushered the affection out the door. Their wife's reactions can be coping mechanisms and defenses that she places around her heart to make her feel safe.

It doesn't make much sense to withhold the necessary elements a plant needs (like air, water, and soil) and then blame the plant for not thriving. However, many a man has labeled his wife sexually frigid for not wanting to be touched or have sex. But wives have often told me that when they are mistreated, they feel like prostitutes having physical relations with their husbands. Sex is more than just physical—it involves every part of us. A woman must first know she is valued as a person and be in harmony with her husband before she can give herself freely in sex. She has to feel romantic love before *wholeheartedly* entering the sexual union in marriage. Without harmony, the sexual relationship between husband and wife will most certainly deteriorate. Do you want to experience the best sex of your life? Do you believe that sex ten, twenty, thirty years into marriage can be better than the honeymoon? It can. The bedroom is a barometer of the marriage. A hot loving relationship translates into hot sex.

Have you ever known the futility of trying to reach a woman mentally, emotionally, or physically after offending her? Mark tried to reach out to Laurie, his estranged wife, but she wanted no part of him. He kept saying to her, "I miss you so much. I want to be near you. I love you." But she was *closed* to him emotionally. "Don't you see how you're hurting our daughter?" he said. "Don't you see what kind of reputation we're going to have by being separated?" He tried to appeal to her mentally, but she wouldn't listen. He had already gone too far—he had offended her too often and too severely—so her spirit completely shut him out of her life.

I asked him, "Are you willing to forgo touching Laurie for the time being, to forgo wondering if she will ever again have emotional feelings for you, to forgo trying to reason with her mentally? Will you first concentrate on clearing up your past offenses? If you will accept my counsel and reestablish harmony with Laurie, she will mentally open up to you again. She'll gain new romantic love for you. Finally, she will desire to be near you again.

"This is the reality of life," I advised Mark. "In cases where a woman has fallen in love with another man or has been severely mistreated, it may take longer to win her back."

A man often becomes disgusted when his wife doesn't sparkle with romance anymore, not realizing that he killed that sparkle with his hurtful ways. So what steps can a man take to rebuild a harmonious relationship with his wife?

Identify the Ways You May Have Hurt Your Wife

To help you avoid hurting your mate, I have included a list of ways a husband commonly offends his wife. Go through the list and see if you can identify some of the ways you have failed your wife in the past. If you need help, you have an expert in your own home — your wife. Calmly and gently ask your wife to identify some of the problem areas as well, and listen carefully to her answer. You may be amazed at how well she remembers your unloving words and actions. Hearing her words and seeing the list in black and white may help you realize how offensive these behaviors are and how deeply your actions can wound her.

1. Ignoring her.
2. Not valuing her opinions.
3. Showing more attention to other people than to her.
4. Not listening to her or not understanding what she feels is important.
5. Closing her out by not talking or listening to her (the silent treatment).
6. Being easily distracted when she's trying to talk.

7. Not scheduling special time to be with her.

8. Not being open to talk about things that you do not understand.

9. Not being open to talk about things that she does not understand.

10. Not giving her a chance to voice her opinion on decisions that affect the whole family.

11. Disciplining her by avoiding her.

12. Making jokes about areas of her life.

13. Making sarcastic statements about her.

14. Insulting her in front of others.

15. Coming back with quick retorts.

16. Giving harsh admonitions.

17. Using careless words before you think through how they will affect her.

18. Nagging her in harshness.

19. Rebuking her before giving her a chance to explain a situation.

20. Raising your voice at her.

21. Making critical comments with no logical basis.

22. Swearing or using foul language in her presence.

23. Correcting her in public.

24. Being tactless when pointing out her weaknesses or blind spots.

25. Reminding her angrily that you warned her not to do something.

26. Having disgusted or judgmental attitudes.

27. Pressuring her when she is already feeling low or offended.

28. Lecturing her when she needs to be comforted, encouraged, or treated gently.

29. Breaking promises without any explanation or without being asked to be released from the promise.

30. Telling her how wonderful other women are and comparing her to other women.

31. Holding resentment about something she did and tried to make right.

32. Being disrespectful to her family and relatives.

33. Coercing her into an argument.

34. Correcting or punishing her in anger for something for which she's not guilty.

35. Not praising her for something she did well, even if she did it for you.

36. Treating her like a little child.

37. Being rude to her or to other people in public, like restaurant personnel or clerks.

38. Being unaware of her needs.

39. Being ungrateful.

40. Not trusting her.

41. Not approving of what she does or how she does it.

42. Not being interested in her personal growth.

43. Being inconsistent or having double standards (doing things you don't want her to do).

44. Not giving her advice when she really needs it and asks for it.

45. Not telling her that you love her.

46. Having prideful and arrogant attitudes in general.

47. Not giving daily encouragement.

48. Failing to include her in a conversation when you are with other people.

49. Failing to spend quantity or quality time with her when you're at a party.

50. "Talking her down"—continuing to discuss or argue a point just to prove you're right.

51. Ignoring her around the house as if she weren't a member of the family.

52. Not taking time to listen to what she believes is important as soon as you come home from work.

53. Ignoring her at social gatherings.

54. Not attending church as a family.

55. Failing to express honestly what you think her innermost feelings are.

56. Showing more excitement for work and other activities than for her.

57. Being impolite at mealtime.

58. Having sloppy manners around the house and in front of others.

59. Not inviting her out on special romantic dates from time to time.

60. Not helping her with the children.

61. Not helping with housework.

62. Making her feel stupid when she shares an idea about your work or decisions that need to be made.

63. Making her feel unworthy for desiring certain furniture or other material needs for herself and the family.

64. Not spending quality and quantity time with the children.

65. Not showing public affection for her, like holding her hand or putting your arm around her (you seem to be embarrassed to be with her).

66. Not sharing your life with her, like your ideas or your feelings (e.g., what's going on at work).

67. Not being the spiritual leader of the home.

68. Demanding that she submit to you.

69. Demanding that she have sex even when you are not in harmony.

70. Being unwilling to admit you were wrong.

71. Getting defensive whenever she shares one of your "blind spots."

72. Being too busy with work and activities.

73. Not showing compassion and understanding for her and the children when there is real need.

74. Not planning for the future, making her very insecure.

75. Being stingy with money, making her feel like she's being paid a salary—and not much at all.

76. Wanting to do things that embarrass her sexually.

77. Consuming porn privately or in front of her.

78. Forcing her to make many of the decisions regarding the budget.

79. Forcing her to handle bill collectors and overdue bills.

80. Not letting her lean on your gentleness and strength from time to time.

81. Not allowing her to fail—always feeling like you have to lecture her.

82. Refusing to let her be a woman.

83. Criticizing her womanly characteristics or sensitivity as being weak.

84. Spending too much money and getting the family too far into debt.

85. Not having a sense of humor and not joking about things together.

86. Not telling her how important she is to you.

87. Not sending her special love letters, emails, or texts from time to time.

88. Forgetting or not celebrating special dates like anniversaries and birthdays.

89. Not defending her when somebody else is tearing her down (especially if it's one of your relatives or friends).

90. Not putting your arm around her and hugging her when she's in need of comfort.

91. Not bragging to other people about her.

92. Being dishonest.

93. Discouraging her from trying to better herself, either through education or physical fitness.

94. Continuing distasteful or harmful habits, like coming home drunk.

95. Not treating her as if "Handle with Care" were stamped on her forehead.

96. Ignoring her relatives and the people who are important to her.

97. Taking her for granted.

98. Not including her in future plans until the last minute.

99. Never doing little unexpected things for her.

100. Not treating her like an intellectual equal.

101. Looking at her as a weaker individual in general.

102. Being preoccupied with your own goals and needs, making her feel like she and the children do not count.

103. Threatening never to let her do something again because she made some mistake in the past.

104. Criticizing her behind her back. (This is really painful for her if she hears about your criticism from someone else.)

105. Blaming her for things in your relationship that are clearly your fault.

106. Not being aware of her physical limitations, treating her like a man by roughhousing with her or making her carry heavy objects.

107. Losing patience or getting angry with her when she can't keep up with your schedule or physical stamina.

108. Acting like you're a martyr if you go along with her opinions.

109. Sulking when she challenges your comments.

110. Joining too many organizations that exclude her and the children.

111. Failing to repair items around the house.

112. Watching too much TV or spending too much time on the computer and therefore neglecting her and the children.

113. Demanding that she sit and listen to your point of view when she needs to be taking care of the children's needs.

114. Insisting on lecturing her in order to convey what you believe are important points.

115. Humiliating her with words and actions, saying things like "I can't stand living in a pigpen."

116. Not taking the time to prepare her to enjoy sexual intimacy.

117. Spending money extravagantly without helping those less fortunate.

118. Avoiding family activities that the children enjoy.

119. Taking vacations that are primarily for your pleasure, like fishing or hunting, while preventing her from doing the things she enjoys doing.

120. Not letting her get away from the children just to be with friends, go shopping for special items, or have a weekend away with her friends.

121. Being unwilling to join her in the things she enjoys.

122. Not appreciating some of the more mundane chores she may handle, like picking up clothes and toys, wiping runny noses, washing and ironing, grocery shopping, and so forth.

Understand the Hurt You Have Caused

Persistent disharmony is almost always reduced by you sincerely endeavoring to understand the ways you have offended your wife—literally trying to understand the depth of the hurt she has felt by your actions. The greater your understanding of her suffering, the easier it can be for you to see what you've done wrong.

Let's stop here. Would you mind if I paused to emphasize how important understanding is? *Understanding* a woman's feelings is more than half of the battle to restore harmony and return to a happier marriage. To help you increase your understanding of her emotions, ask her to try to use as many word pictures as she can to help describe how she feels. Here are some examples of what she might say:

"I feel like a baby bird in a nest and I spot a snake slithering toward me."

"What you said to me yesterday has left me feeling like a dog who has been run over by a car and I can't get up by myself. I need your arms around me gently lifting me off of the road."

"On a zero to ten scale of hurt, I'm at an eight right now."

Have her use word pictures from nature, your personal history, the Bible, science, or whatever helps you better understand how she is feeling. Understanding and being able to feel what your wife feels is so necessary before you do the next difficult step—admitting your part in weakening your marriage.

Admit Your Part in Weakening Your Marriage

Ken and Sharon's story is a good example of how a man's insensitivity can damage a marriage. After eight years of marriage and three children, Sharon's once-petite figure was a little on the chubby side. Since Ken couldn't understand why she had not regained her slender figure after the birth of their third child, he found a number of "creative" ways to point out the extra poundage to Sharon. He tried to make her lose weight by lecturing, demanding, and bribing. He even threatened to cancel their vacation unless she lost weight. But nothing worked. She seemed powerless to comply.

Ken's continually critical, harsh attitude wounded Sharon. As a result, she slowly began to close him out of her life. She shut him out emotionally and resisted when he demanded sex, excusing herself because of headaches or fatigue. His occasional jabs, "Do you realize you had two desserts for dinner tonight?" and his overbearing personality continually pressured her, making her more nervous and increasing her desire to eat. Ken was totally unaware of what he was doing to her. "If you want to lose weight," he said, "you just decide to do it!" Ken had no idea that scolding an addicted person merely increases their addiction. In fact, my son, Dr. Greg Smalley, a psychologist, has discovered in his marriage research that the key to any marriage relationship becoming more loving and healthy is for each partner to feel safe. When a mate feels offended and nothing is done to repair the damage, the mate may continue to feel unsafe and the marriage declines.

Since Sharon had little or no interest in pleasing Ken, she might have been subconsciously punishing him by staying overweight. Quite by accident, Ken did one thing that finally motivated Sharon to lose weight. He called her long distance while on a business trip and said, "Honey, as I've been away from you and the kids these past few days, I've had a lot of time to think. I know I've never been able to face it before, but I've been judgmental and offensive to each of you. In fact, I can see now that *I've* been the one out of control. In many ways, my crummy, hurtful attitude is worse than anything you've done to me.

"What I plan to do is to stop pestering you about losing weight and to spend the rest of my life focusing on how I can work on being a better friend and husband. I want to concentrate on learning how to love you for who you are, not criticizing you for not measuring up to my standards. My actions are far worse than anything I'm criticizing you for. I want you to know that you're free from demands from me to change and that I love you just the way you are."

After a few stunned seconds, Sharon responded, "You know, every time you demanded that I lose weight, your attitude made me want to run to the refrigerator and eat everything in it! I never had any desire to please you in this area. But now that you say I'm free to do whatever I want and I sense you mean it, I actually have a greater desire to lose weight" — which she did by losing over seventy pounds in the next few months.

When Ken began to recognize that his criticism was wounding his wife, he was on the path to a restored relationship. This is a perfect example of what I have learned late in life (almost too late). Personal responsibility is about focusing on the only person you can change: *you*. It is getting off of your mate's case and working on *your own* heart and life.

Men, I want you to keep in mind that this whole book is directed to *you*. It's not intended for a woman to read, and it doesn't specifically apply to what she needs to do to restore or rebuild a relationship. I've taken the time to write an entire book for her, *For Better or for Best*, to point out areas where her attitudes and actions can serve to strengthen or weaken your marriage.

What you're about to read may be very difficult for you to believe or even accept, but consider it carefully: If your marriage is continually under stress, filled with strife, and is bordering on collapse, you've been participating in weakening it.

But there's a principle that's even harder to swallow. When I first heard what you're about to read, I squirmed and fought and argued against the whole idea for at least a month. I want you to experience whatever emotions are natural to you as you read the statement below. If you react strongly, I understand why. In spite of my initial opposition, I ultimately realized that there was more truth in it than I wanted to admit. You may want to react like I did and spend long hours trying to disprove it. But let's face it together.

If a couple has been married for more than five years, all of the *husband's* emotional unhappiness is 100 percent his fault.

In other words, your feelings of unhappiness in your marriage are directly traceable to the beliefs you have placed within your own heart. And to transform your emotions, you can only work on one person: yourself. I hated hearing this truth at first. But now, I love it.

After thirty-eight years of marriage, I finally started living out this concept because of the confrontation and encouragement of my own son. Greg walked into our house one day when I was attempting to "help" Norma improve one of her "bad" habits so she would "stop ruining or weakening our marriage." She was responding to me as she usually did to these conversations, by disconnecting and placing distance between us.

Greg pulled me aside to talk out in the front yard. "Dad, when will you be willing to listen to my research with couples that says you can't change your wife or your marriage by going head to head with her?"

"Well," I said, "who can help her if I can't?"

"How about letting God give it a try?" he asked.

I got offended. "Don't spiritualize this!" I told him.

"The point is, Dad," he said, "no one can change another person. You can only change yourself. If you continue trying to change Mom, you are injecting the biggest killer of marriages: an unsafe place. When a persons feels safe in the presence of their mate, they will automatically open their heart, and the best type of deep, loving friendship happens almost without effort. But when couples feel unsafe with each other, they will separate in every way. It starts with thoughts of withdrawal, then words, then actions, and finally they become emotionally dead. They can't even remember why they married in the first place."

So I swallowed my pride and tried his advice as a scientific study of one. I invited Norma to dinner and apologized for offending her for thirty-eight years. I pledged to stop working on her and instead to work on my own heart and life. And I followed through on that pledge.

As a result, I've seen bigger and healthier changes within my life over the past eight years than I experienced in my first sixty-two years. My life and marriage have been transformed. And Norma has thrived. Not only has she changed the two areas that most irritated me in our marriage, she is at seventy a beautiful woman with a lot of laughter and drive to keep working at our company.

My own son taught me that when you concentrate on what *you* can do to improve your marriage, your wife will change in response to *your* changes. And I've never met a woman who stays grumpy, negative, or unresponsive to a man when he is loving, caring, and highly honoring her. When a woman feels valuable to a man and when she sees him trying hard to understand her and care for her, she will respond favorably. If you get your eyes off of seeing her negative behavior and pick on yourself and find out how *you* can change, you won't believe the positive changes that will come to her and your marriage.

Express Genuine Sorrow When You Offend Your Wife

Your wife is far too valuable to treat in a dishonoring way, so whenever you offend her, express genuine sorrow for your offense. When she is convinced that you are sincere, reconciliation is possible. If your sorrow is not sincere, beware. You have only increased your offense.

One of the most dramatic examples of the power of this particular point was shown to me by an All-Pro defensive player on an NFL championship team.

At a professional football conference where I was speaking, I walked into the coffee shop and witnessed this player and his wife in the middle of a very tense and tearful discussion. Knowing how big and powerful these athletes are—especially when they're angry—I was a little reluctant when he called me over to the table and asked if I would talk with them for a few minutes.

He had been upset with his wife because she was too tired after their long airplane flight to go out with some friends after the evening meeting. Her reluctance displeased him, and he shamed her in front of the other couple. He was angry with her all night too. Now, over breakfast, he was trying to make up and she wasn't responding.

When they walked into the coffee shop, he tried to put his arm around her, and she pulled away, embarrassing him in the process. Before they knew it, they were in the middle of another fight. That's when he called me over to the table.

"I don't want to spend the whole week like this. What can we do?" he said.

I encouraged him to understand how hurtful it was for her to hear his harsh put-downs in front of the other players and wives.

And he said, "Well, it was wrong of her too. She could have stayed up for another hour. We're at a conference, and this is a place to have fun!"

Then she said, "This is so typical. He's always thinking about having fun with his friends and doesn't really care about me. I was tired from getting us packed and the kids off to my folks, and he got mad because he didn't want to go without me."

The tension level between the two of them was so high by this point that it could have reheated the coffee in front of us. Other people seated around us were painfully aware of the scene between them.

I tried something with them that I had never done before (nor since), and the immediate results amazed all of us. I said to the husband, "If you don't want to be upset all week, would you be willing to do something like this? For just a minute, let me pretend that I'm you." Then I asked him to pay attention to what I was about to say to his wife.

I reached across the table, and I put my hand gently on top of hers. I looked her right in the eyes and I said in a soft voice, "What I said to you in front of our friends last night was really wrong. I know it embarrassed you and really offended you. You're just too valuable to be treated like this. In fact, I don't even know how you put up with me like you do. You may not be able to respond right now, and I'll try to understand if you can't, but if you could, I'd love it if you forgave me. I know I don't deserve it, and I know I may blow it again. But I want you to know with all my heart that I don't want to hurt you, and I don't like living this way."

I pulled my hand away and sat back. Immediately, tears welled up in her eyes, and her facial muscles and her entire body seemed to relax.

"Do you see what's happening to your wife here?" I asked my NFL friend. As he looked at her, tears began to show in his eyes as well, and I said to him, "Can you see how your wife would respond if you would treat her with tenderness and be willing to admit the times that you're wrong?"

She immediately turned to him and said, "Yeah, but you could never do that!"

"Oh, yes I could," he said in an irritated tone of voice. Almost instantly he was on the defensive, and her facial muscles tightened up again.

For the next hour and a half he practiced—with his arm around her or gently holding her hand—how to speak to her and ask her forgiveness in a soft, genuine way when he had wronged her. On the football field, this fellow had spent years learning to "never give an inch." Now he began to discover that in marriage, when he wronged his wife he needed to take off the shoulder pads and admit that he was wrong. Two years later, I saw this same couple at another conference, and their marriage had never been better because of practicing this one principle.

My wife, Norma, has told me time and time again how much she appreciates seeing my genuine sorrow when I have hurt her. "How do you put up with me? How do you live with me? You deserve the medal of honor for staying with me. You deserve the purple heart. You are an amazing woman to live with such an insensitive man." Sincere words like those express my repentant spirit and soothe our relationship.

I asked one woman, "After your husband has verbally abused you, would you appreciate it if he admitted he was wrong and expressed sorrow that you were hurting? What would you do if he said, 'How do you put up with such a crumb like me, as insensitive as I am?'"

"I'd call the cops," she said.

I repeated in amazement, "You'd call the cops?"

"Yes, because I'd know that there was an imposter in the house," she replied.

I have had wives say to me, "My husband will never admit when he's wrong. He's too proud." Yet I meet husbands everywhere who are willing to admit their offenses if their wives are patient enough to help them understand *how* they have offended them. If your wife is unwilling to show you how you have hurt her, you might have wounded her too deeply for her to trust you with this intimate information for fear you will use it against her. In that case, you will need to do the extra work of seeking insight from a counselor or pastor or close friend who can help you pinpoint the error in your ways. But even if you don't know precisely what you have done wrong, you can *still* show genuine concern and sorrow when you can see that your wife is hurt or offended.

Seek Her Forgiveness for Your Offensive Behavior

A woman needs a man who *understands* the *depth* of her grief after his hurtful behavior. Wives have said to me, "If only my husband knew how much I feel those words that he says so glibly and harshly. If only he knew how long they stay with me." Harsh words can stay with a woman for years.

One of my favorite speaking experiences took place at a Promise Keepers event back in the nineties at a stadium in Indianapolis, Indiana. There were about sixty thousand men in attendance. I asked every man to take one shoe off and pull one strand of hair from his head. Then I asked them to drop the hair on the floor. "Did you hear anything," I asked them.

"No!" they shouted.

"Okay, now drop your shoe." A loud roar filled the stadium. "Did you hear that shoe fall?" I asked.

"Yes!" they roared.

"That's the difference between you and your wife!" I said.

Silence. The men were wondering what I meant.

"Guys," I said, "a lot of the words you use with your wife or your actions toward her seem like no big deal, about the size of a strand of hair. But she experiences them like sixty thousand shoes falling in a stadium. You may not understand why your wife is lying on the floor in tears because one hair can't possibly hurt her. Oh, yes it does, because God designed the typical female to be very sensitive and very aware of what is going on around her, and what to you seems like one hair to her seems like sixty thousand shoes."

A woman loves to hear her man say, "Will you forgive me?" And when she verbalizes, "Yes, you're forgiven," she is freer to restore her side of the relationship. However, if her husband simply says, "Oh, honey, I'm sorry," it's not always enough. He might be able to get away with it if he says it in a tender and gentle way, but a woman really needs to hear, "Will you forgive me?" That proves her husband values her half of the relationship. A flippant "I'm sorry" may mean "I'm sorry I got caught," or, "I'm sorry to have to put up with your sensitivity." It usually doesn't restore the relationship to oneness and harmony.

Initially, your wife may appear unable or unwilling to grant forgiveness for any number of reasons. Perhaps she doesn't really believe you, or she thinks you really don't *understand* her real hurts or disappointment. She may even bluntly say, "No, I won't forgive you ..." or, "Give me some time ..." or, "When I see a change in you, *maybe* ..." All of these are responses of a woman who has been deeply hurt, and all of them might tempt you to react in anger or try to attack her verbally for not forgiving you.

As hard as it may be to restrain yourself, reacting in anger to her statements can only drive her further away. Very often, a woman needs a track record of demonstrated sorrow before emotionally feeling like granting forgiveness to her husband. She may make the decision to forgive, but it may take her some time to feel forgiving. That's why husbands need to be aware of something unique about women.

Most women respond to a husband who genuinely and *persistently* seeks to restore their relationship. It may take an hour or several hours of cooling off and then coming back to talk. But like the situation of the NFL football player, a wife will usually respond positively to a man who gently and persistently asks her forgiveness. And that is why the next point is so important.

Sincerely Work to Change Your Ways

Finally, let your wife see your consistent and sincere efforts to correct offensive actions or words. This is another way of saying, "Repent." For the Greeks, the word *repent* literally meant "to turn around." It means that you are to change your way of thinking or acting to the way Christ thought and acted (Luke 17:3–5).

God called the man to be the leader in nurturing his wife and children. If he leads in offensive, harsh, angry behavior, he will reap the results in a weakened or fractured marriage. But if he leads with a positive tone and a gentle and loving spirit, he will reap positive benefits.

Just listen to this husband who deeply offended his wife and had no idea what he had done. She divorced him and he had no clue why.

"She was always the main problem, right from the beginning," Mike told me.

"Were you at fault at all?" I asked.

"No, I had nothing to do with it! Take this one example," he said, confident that he could show me that his wife was really messed up from the start. "On our wedding night we had sexual relations. She was turned off by the whole experience and from that day on, for over twenty years, she never really enjoyed our sex life. She never initiated it. She didn't even want to be involved. She was more like one of those life-size sex dolls from Hollywood than a living, breathing person. How would I be the cause of that? On our wedding night, she changed on me!"

Mike had dated Carol for three years. So I asked how he treated her during those years.

"Well, okay," he said.

"Mike, I happen to know that it wasn't okay. You and I both know that you had a reputation of being mean and extremely insensitive to her. Do you remember some of the things you did?"

When he admitted that he did remember, I said, "You really hurt her feelings. During all those years that you dated her, did you ever clear up your offenses with her?"

"No, I didn't. I didn't know how to do it. I didn't know what to do," he said.

"Why did she marry you—to get away from her family?"

"Right."

"Then the first night she realized that sex wasn't that great. And do you know why?" I asked. "Because you two weren't in harmony. Besides this fact, did you prepare her for sex?" I explained that many women tell me they need as much as three days' preparation for sex, romantically and emotionally, before they can respond to their husbands. Men are microwaves, women are crock-pots. She *warms up* to the sexual expression, while he *turns on* immediately.

"Did you ever clear your conscience with her? Did you ever clear those past offenses when you were married?" I asked him.

"No, I never did." Mike had never admitted he was wrong.

"Did you criticize your wife a lot?" I asked.

Mike's head sank lower and lower. "I'm ashamed to tell you this, but I told her on our first night together sexually that we needed to keep the lights off. I didn't like her body. I didn't say it, but she figured it out by the way I said it. That started us off with a major blunder! And to make matters worse, I once told her all our problems were her fault." After a few minutes, tears appeared in his eyes because he realized how insensitive, cruel, and harsh he had been for all those years.

Through counseling, Mike finally began to realize his part in destroying their marriage. I had to role play with him many times so he could gain an understanding of Carol's feelings. I also showed him how to share his grief over what he had done and said to her. Eventually Mike went to Carol and humbly admitted his fault, then carefully listened to her when she expressed how she had felt during their marriage. It took over a year, but amazingly, Carol began dating Mike again. He kept at it and never gave up on her, mainly because he didn't want her to keep all of the bitterness within her heart. That was selfless love!

A woman isn't impressed with a man who seeks forgiveness or admits he is wrong and then continues to hurt her year after year in the same areas. Words are nice, but they are not enough. When I sought forgiveness from Norma for offending her hundreds of times when I would attempt to teach her how to live a healthier lifestyle, she easily forgave me after several months of demonstrating that I got off of her case for good. Our wives must see real changes in us, and real change comes faster for the average man when he concentrates on changing *himself* first and waiting and watching for corresponding changes in his wife.

Attitudes, not words or actions, often harm a woman the most. When she *sees* her husband's attitudes changing, she is more willing to hope again and to be open with him and accept him into an intimate relationship. Otherwise, she'll keep him closed off for fear of being offended again.

A Major Exception

After more than forty years of working with couples all across the country, I have discovered only one situation that makes it more difficult and, in some very rare cases, nearly impossible for a wife to respond to her husband's genuine love when he consistently applies it.

This situation arises when a woman has had prolonged anger in her life. She has spent years being bitter and resentful toward her mom and dad or others, and as a result she has developed into a habitual liar and someone who has deep-seated feelings of inferiority. These three deadly ingredients—unresolved resentment, habitual lying, and deep-seated inferiority—can create what M. Scott Peck calls a "person of the lie." These people seem to be unwilling to remember their own deep pain from past hurts or recognize and deal with the hurts they cause others, and they steadfastly refuse to admit any wrong in their own lives. They tend to blame everyone but themselves for their problems. This type of person can "suck the soul right out of others." People feel manipulated in their presence. This person is capable of becoming an evil character.

But remember, it is most unusual for a wife to be unresponsive to her husband's sincere love. People of the lie are very rare. Before you jump to any conclusions or say to yourself, "Now that's better. He's finally talking about my wife," look at some of the ways that a husband can offend his wife and can contribute to her developing anger, resentment, or other negative emotions or behavior. The charts on the following pages can show you how your own bad behavior may be weakening your marriage. The charts were devised by Ken Nair, a marriage and family lecturer/counselor.

How a Husband's Lack of Genuine Love
Weakens a Marriage

HUSBAND'S ACTIONS

Husband's Lack of Genuine Love	*Amplified*
UNRELIABLE	Lets time slip by unnoticed.
UNTRUSTING AND CONDEMNING	Has an attitude of superiority in finances. Demands the control of all money. Won't let his wife know about their financial status. Fells certain his wife would bankrupt him if she were given the chance.
ANGRY AND DEMANDING	In anger, overreacts to children and others. Doesn't like to be inconvenienced by family. Sets standards too difficult for children to meet.
INSENSITIVE AND UNKIND	Uses hurtful words to others. Uses his wife or others as his source of humor.
INATTENTIVE, THOUGHTLESS, AND UNTRUSTWORTHY	Preoccupied with personal concerns. Dismisses other's personal feeling as unrealistic or invalid—if he acknowledges them at all. Family's reputation has been damaged by his lack of consideration for others.
UNCARING AND IRRESPONSIBLE	Doesn't seem to care about his family's needs. Seems to think the only obligation he has to the family is financial.

RESULT	**WIFE'S RESPONSES**
Wife's Offensive Habits	*Amplified*
NAGGING	Repeatedly reminds her husband about things that need attention, with illustrations of his past wrongs and forgetfulness.
IMPULSIVE SPENDER	Spends money as though it were very easily obtained. Seems irresponsible with money when it comes into her possession. Uses credit cards without concern.
PERMISSIVE WITH CHILDREN	Makes excuses for children's disobedience to husband and keeps secrets from him about their conduct.
TOO EMOTIONAL	Cries often and is easily hurt. Holds on to hurts for a long time. Able to recall past offenses in detail.
DOMINATING	Answers all questions, even those directed to her husband. Makes the decisions in the home and assumes responsibility for disciplining the children.
NAGGING	Repeatedly reminds her husband about things that need attention, with illustrations of his past wrongs and forgetfulness.

Can You Identify with Any of These Typical Conflicts in Marriage?

1. She wants to be with her mother more than with you
2. She's lazy
3. She's sexually frigid
4. She's sneaky
5. She's overly critical of the way you spend money
6. She avoids doing activities with you
7. She makes you feel like a nobody
8. She's afraid of speaking in front of groups
9. She yells at the kids in the morning
10. She's inflexible, always gets offended
11. She's rebellious (unsubmissive)
12. She's disrespectful of you
13. She's snappy, angry
14. She reacts negatively to your friends
15. She's naggy
16. She's afraid of moving
17. She talks too much on the telephone
18. She's too lenient with the children
19. She reacts negatively to your relatives
20. She's too strict with the children
21. She's unwilling to pray with you

You and I need to become more responsible, loving partners, no matter what our wives do. That is the basis for genuine love — *doing what is right no matter what the other person does or says.* Genuine love motivates us to build a relationship primarily for the other person's sake, and when we do that, *we* gain because we have a better relationship to enjoy.

For Personal Reflection

1. What should we do if our mates offend us (Luke 17:3–4)?
2. What attitude should we have when we rebuke an offender (Galatians 6:1; Proverbs 15:1)?

6

WHAT NO WOMAN
CAN RESIST

■ ■ ■

Let no unwholesome word proceed from your mouth,
but only such a word as is good for edification.

Ephesians 4:29

The crunch of corn chips distracted my attention from the Saturday afternoon football game. I watched in amazement as my wife and three children began to eat their sandwiches and drink their Cokes while I sat only a couple of feet away without a bite to eat.

"Why didn't she make me a sandwich?" I asked myself. "I'm the sole bread winner, and I'm being ignored as if I didn't exist." I cleared my throat loudly to catch my wife's attention. When that didn't work, I became so irritated that I walked into the kitchen, got the bread out, and made my own sandwich. When I sat back down in front of the TV, Norma didn't say a word, nor did I. But I kept wondering, "If women are so sensitive, how come she didn't know I wanted a sandwich? If women are so alert, why didn't she hear me clear my throat or notice that I wasn't speaking to her? Why didn't she notice the expression of irritation on my face?"

A few days later when we were talking calmly, I said, "I've really been wondering about something, but I hesitate asking you this question. I was really intrigued the other day, and I wonder if I could ask you a personal question?" By now I had aroused her curiosity.

"Sure," she said.

"You know last Saturday when I was watching the football game and you made sandwiches for all the kids? Could I ask you why you didn't make one for me?"

"Are you serious?" she asked. She looked at me with such amazement that it really confused me.

"Sure, I'm serious. I would think that since I'm the one who earns all the money for food around here that you would have made me something to eat too."

"You know, I really can't believe that you would even ask a question like that," she said. By now I was thinking, "Maybe I shouldn't have asked. Maybe I should know the answer." It seemed very obvious to her, but it didn't seem obvious to me at all.

"Norma, I really don't see it. I admit I am blind in some areas," I pursued, "and I can see this is one of them. Would you mind telling me?"

"Sometimes women are accused of being stupid, but we aren't," she answered. "We don't just set ourselves up to be criticized." She seemed to think that explained why she hadn't made me a sandwich.

"I can understand that. But what does that have to do with the sandwiches?"

"Do you realize that every time I make you a sandwich, you say something critical about it? 'Norma, you didn't give me enough lettuce ... Is this avocado ripe? You put too much mayonnaise on this. Hey, how about some butter, it's a little dry.' Maybe you've never realized it, but you have had a critical statement for every sandwich I ever made. I just wasn't up to being criticized the other day. It wasn't worth it. I don't enjoy being criticized."

I had egg all over my face because I could recall many times when I had criticized her as she handed me sandwiches. But every time? I wanted to say, "Come on, hon, let's get realistic! Every time?" But instead I remembered that for a woman, "always" and "never" don't mean the same thing as they do to a man when they're spoken with emotion. Norma's tone of voice and facial expression as well as her words were telling me this was something that really bothered her. I was simply eating the fruit of my ways. I sowed criticism and reaped an empty plate. I am happy to say that after that experience I began praising every sandwich she made for me, and now she doesn't hesitate to make them for me. If all she does is butter two pieces of bread and slap them together, I respond with, "This is probably the best sandwich I have ever had!"

The Need for Appreciation

Shortly after Marilyn left Bob, I asked her if she could recall things for which Bob had praised her. She couldn't remember a single time during their twenty-plus years of marriage. Her children confirmed it. They agreed that their mother had never served a single dinner that their father didn't criticize in at least one way. He had complained when the salt and pepper weren't on the table or when she didn't cook the meat just right. She finally reached the point where she didn't even want to be near his critical personality. She left him for another man.

"I'm kind of happy she's leaving me, because she never wants to do anything with me anyway," Bob said. "She's a party-pooper and a loner. She excludes me from her activities. Do you know she never wanted to go on a vacation with me? I've tried and I've tried, but she never wants to. I'm disgusted with her too."

We didn't discuss his marital problems until after he told me about his job change due to friction with his former boss.

"How did he treat you, Bob?" I asked.

"He'd come out to the shop where I was the foreman, and he'd look for one little thing to yell at me about in front of all my men. That really hurt me deeply. Then he would go back to his office, and I'd continue working my fingers to the bone. He'd never notice how hard I worked or even say anything positive about it. I couldn't take it anymore, so I asked for a transfer."

I asked Bob, "Would you take a vacation with your boss?"

"Are you kidding? That would be the worst thing in the world," he answered.

"How about doing other activities with him?"

"No way! He's so critical; he'd even ruin a trip to Hawaii!"

What I told Bob next blew open his mind to finally understand his wife. I pointed out how as a husband he was just like his boss, and his face dropped and tears came to his eyes.

"You're right. No wonder Marilyn never wanted to go anywhere with me. I never think about things she does to please me, and I'm always criticizing her in front of the children and our friends."

But it was too late. Marilyn was already in love with another man. Though Bob changed drastically and is now much more sensitive to women, his wife divorced him and remarried.

Women need praise. We should be able to understand their need because we too want to know that we are of value to other people. One of the ways we know we're needed is when others express appreciation for who we are and what we do.

The Scriptures remind us that our major relationships involve praise:

1. Praising God (Ps. 100:4).

2. Praising our wives (Prov. 31:28).

3. Praising others; for example, our Christian friends (Eph. 4:29).

I can vividly remember my boss saying years ago, "If only I had ten men like you, we could change the world." After that, I was so motivated I couldn't do enough for him.

Teachers know how praise motivates children. One teacher said she praised each student in her third-grade class every day, without exception. Her students were the most motivated, encouraged, and enthusiastic in the school. When my substitute high school geometry teacher praised me regularly, my D average climbed to an A in six weeks.

Knowing how significant praise can be, why do we as husbands fail to express it to our wives? Several reasons. The most common is preoccupation with our own needs, vocation, and activities. We lose sight of the positive and helpful qualities in our wives when we are preoccupied. Even worse, we fail to acknowledge our wives' helpful traits when we do notice them.

When a husband forgets his wife's need for praise, the marriage is usually on its way downhill. And if he constantly expresses the bitter instead of the sweet, his marriage will become less fulfilling every day. Criticism is devastating, especially when voiced in anger or harshness (Prov. 15:1, 4). When a husband rails against his wife for her unique feminine qualities, he conveys a lack of approval for her as a person. This automatically weakens their relationship.

Develop a Positive Attitude

Charlie Jones, in the book *Life Is Tremendous*, says we really can't enjoy life until we learn how to see and say something positive about everything. Though none of us will ever be completely positive about life, he says, we can be in the process of learning, growing, and developing a positive attitude.

If you develop a positive attitude, not only will others want to be around you more often, but your wife will also benefit tremendously. She will have a greater sense of worth and value, knowing you have provided the encouragement only a husband can give.

Praise Your Wife at Least Once a Day

Promise yourself to tell your wife daily what you appreciate about her. Promise yourself—not her—because she might develop expectations and be hurt if you forget. Begin by learning to verbalize your thoughts of appreciation.

Here are some typical statements wives have told me they enjoy hearing:

1. "What a meal! M-m-m-m ... that was delicious."
2. (This next one is great with an early-morning kiss.) "Honey, I sure love you. You're special to me."
3. While in the company of friends say, "This is *my* wife. She's the greatest!"
4. Put little notes on the refrigerator like, "I loved the way you looked last night."
5. "Our kids are really blessed to have a mother like you. You take such good care of them."
6. "I don't know if I prefer the dress or what's in it better."
7. "Do I like your hairstyle? I'd like any hairstyle you have just because it's on you."
8. "I'd love to take you out tonight just to show you off."
9. "Honey, you've worked so hard. Why don't you sit down and rest for a while before dinner?"
10. "You're so special to me that I'd like to do something special for you right now. Why don't you take a bubble bath and relax. I'll do up the dishes and get the kids started on their homework."
11. "You work hard every day. Thanks for saving me some of your energy. I love how you balance your life!"

In her book *Forever My Love*, Margaret Hardisty emphasized that women tend to approach life on an emotional plane while men approach it on a more logical, sometimes coldly objective one. Therefore, when you praise your wife, it's important to use words and actions that communicate praise from her point of view. Anything that is romantic or deals with building deeper relationships usually pleases wives.

Be Creative with Your Praise

One husband won his wife back partly through creative praise. He bought 365 pieces of wrapped candy, wrote a special message on every wrapper, and then sealed them again. She opened one piece every day and read what he appreciated about her for a full year.

A woman loves to find hidden notes — in her jewelry box, the silver drawer, the medicine cabinet.... Search for ways to praise your wife. Post some compliments on your Facebook wall for your friends to see. Text her throughout the day. Email her. The possibilities are endless.

What kind of praise would you like to hear from your boss? Try a little of it on your wife. You may say, "Well, I don't need too much praise. I'm secure in my job, and I really don't need it." Then interview some of those who work with you to see how they would appreciate being praised. Some of their ideas might work with your wife. Also, ask your wife what kind of praise she likes to hear.

Don't Draw Attention to Your Wife's Unattractive Features

Wrinkles, gray hair, and excess weight are definitely not on the list of possible conversation starters. Even your casual comments about them can make your wife insecure — she may fear being traded in for a "newer model." She knows divorce is just too easy and common nowadays.

One husband wrote his wife a cute poem about how much he

loved her little wrinkles and how he loved caressing her "cellulose cells." Can you say, "Clueless!" His card, though softened with flowers, made her cry for hours. Men, we have to praise our wives without drawing attention to what they believe are their unattractive features.

That doesn't mean you should use insincere flattery. Have you ever been to a party where someone compliments you and you know inside he or she doesn't mean what they say? Sometimes a husband will casually remark, "Oh, yeah, I really like that dress." But his wife can generally detect his insincerity. Even if you don't like her dress, you can say something sincere like, "Honey, that color makes you look ten years younger."

Look on the Positive Side

Did you know you can even find something to praise in your wife's faults? The chart *How to Find the Positive Side of Your Wife's "Negative" Traits* can get you started on finding the positive aspects in the things you consider her "flaws."

How to Find the Positive Side to Your Wife's "Negative" Traits

Negative	Positive
Nosy	She may be very *alert* or *sociable.*
Touchy	She may be very *sensitive.*
Manipulative	She may be a very *resourceful* or *perceptive* person.
Stingy	She may be very *thrifty.*
Talkative	She may be very *expressive* and *dramatic.*
Flighty	She may be an *enthusiastic* person with *cheerful vitality.*
Too serious	She may be a very *sincere* and *earnest* person.

Too bold	She may have *strong convictions*.
Rigid	She may be a *well-disciplined* person with *high standards*.
Overbearing	She may be a very *confident* person — sure of herself.
A dreamer	She may be very *creative* and *imaginative*.
Too fussy	She may be very *organized* and *efficient*.

Make Your Praise Detailed and Specific

Specific praise is far better than *general* praise. For example, "That was a great dinner" doesn't do nearly as much for her as, "The asparagus with the nutmeg sauce was fantastic. I've never had asparagus that tasted so good. I don't know how you can take plain, ordinary vegetables and turn them into such mouth-watering delights."

"You're a great mom" won't send her into orbit, but this might: "I'm really grateful that I married a woman who is so sensitive that she knows just the perfect way of making our kids feel important. They're sure lucky to have such a sensitive mother."

There is no right or wrong time to praise your wife. She'll love it when you're alone or when you're with the children and friends. Make sure you don't limit your praise to public or private times. If you only praise her in public, she might suspect you're showing off for your friends. If you only praise her in private, she may feel you're embarrassed about doing it in public. Let your praise be a banner of love over her that announces her specialness to everyone you meet (Song of Solomon 2:4).

Whenever you praise her, it's important that your full attention be on her. If she senses that your mind or feelings are elsewhere, your praise will be less meaningful to her.

As you learn how to praise your wife genuinely and consistently, you'll begin to see a new sparkle in her eyes and new life in your relationship.

For Personal Reflection

1. How do we develop a general positive attitude? See 1 Thessalonians 5:16–18; Romans 8:28; James 1:2–3; Hebrews 12:11, 15.

2. What does praising God show us about our relationship with Him (Psalm 100:4)?

7

ASK HOW YOU CAN
IMPROVE AS A HUSBAND

■ ■ ■

*Reprove a wise man
and he will love you.*

Proverbs 9:8

"I'm quitting on Monday," Jim yelled as he blasted through the front door. "My boss finally did it—I'm not working for him anymore!"

Elaine greeted him quietly and listened to her husband's outburst of anger. Giving him time and her full attention, Elaine let Jim vent his frustration. Then when he had poured it all out, she began to help him rethink the situation. She reminded him that he could never replace the ideal working conditions or the six-figure income. Soon Jim had changed his mind. Since then, he has told me it was the best decision he ever made. Today he enjoys his job more than ever.

When Jim *honored* Elaine's advice—when he gave high value to her input—he not only made a wise vocational decision but also a wise marital decision. Her respect and admiration for him greatly increased in response to his openness to her gentle correction.

The proverb that honor follows humility is still true today (Prov. 15:33). And even more significant is the truth that the man who regards reproof will be honored (Prov. 13:18). Humility is an inner attitude that is evidenced by an openness to the ideas and suggestions of others. It is the recognition that we are not all-knowing, that we can make mistakes, that we can always gain more knowledge and understanding.

Listen and Learn!

The inability to accept advice from others can destroy a relationship. Larry had to learn the hard way to take his wife's correction seriously.

Lynn had tried for ten years to explain to Larry how badly he made her feel, but Larry simply couldn't understand. His first problem was preferring his relatives over his wife. Whenever he and Lynn were around his family, he expected her to change her schedule to fit in with his family's. It didn't matter what she had planned. To make matters worse, Larry always took their side and defended them during arguments.

Larry also had a habit of making more commitments than he was able to fulfill—a promise here and a promise there. He was often guilty of forgetting his commitments. He didn't mean any harm. In fact, his intentions were good. He wanted so much to make people happy that he couldn't say no when asked to do something.

Year after year, Lynn tried to think of creative ways to point out these two problems to Larry, but nothing seemed to get through to him. Finally during one particularly straining visit to their hometown, Lynn broke down and cried. She openly expressed dislike for his relatives, bringing on Larry's lectures and retaliation. Neither of them could handle the emotional scene, so Larry drove the car to a parking lot. He sat there for nearly an hour, trying to understand the problem, but he simply couldn't. Larry and Lynn tried to discuss their problem once again as they began the long drive home. Lynn finally hit just the right combination of words that made sense to Larry.

"Oh, so that's why you don't like my relatives," he said. "Now I see why you don't want to move back to our hometown. When we're with my relatives, I always choose their feelings over yours. You feel second-rate. That makes sense now." Lynn was thrilled. The secret to great listening is repeating back what your wife is saying in your own words, tone, and posture. It may take a little back and forth, but when your wife sees that you understand, harmony is near.

One problem down, one to go. But Larry remained just as blind to the second problem as he had been to the first. Though Lynn tried to tell him, he finally had to learn it from his friends through a very painful experience. Six of his buddies called a special meeting to tell him about his problem with overcommitment. They had all suffered from his neglect. Graphically, yet lovingly, they explained to Larry that his inability to say no was causing them to be resentful toward him. Larry was straining his friendship with each of them. He was so embarrassed and humiliated by this two-hour meeting that his first thought was, "Why didn't I listen to Lynn?"

His wife was relieved to see that he finally understood his second major problem. Her respect for him automatically increased because of his willingness to improve once he finally comprehended his faults. He became eager to expend the effort and study necessary to learn how to love Lynn (and others) properly.

Decide to Be Wise

Let's set some goals: that we as husbands decide to be wise and open ourselves to correction (Prov. 9:8–9). And that we be willing to listen to the lessons in each chapter of this book, however painful or difficult, and with our new knowledge, commit ourselves to building better marriages. A better marriage doesn't just happen. It takes serious effort channeled in the right direction. The basic principles presented in each chapter, taken one at a time, will correct or prevent the most serious pitfalls we face in marriage.

Some of us entered marriage with an extremely limited knowledge of how to develop a fulfilling relationship with our wives. But it's not hopeless. With a great deal of teaching and patience on the part of our wives, we can learn. A man needs to take an honest inventory to *assess* where he is in his marriage and be able to *admit* that he might have a long way to go. Your wife can certainly help with that inventory and suggest corrections.

If I'm Open to My Wife's Correction, Do I Give Up Being the Leader?

A husband may resist being open to correction from his wife because he feels it somehow negates his position as the leader of the home. If he listens to his wife's complaints or suggestions to improve their relationship and acts on them, he fears it means letting his wife make every decision or giving up control of the home.

I've noticed that almost without exception, the same man who has so much difficulty accepting correction from his wife also struggles with accepting correction from others. Not only that, but he is usually an expert at criticizing his spouse for her many faults.

Without question, the Scriptures call the man to be the leader and head of the home. Yet like Christ, we are to lead in love—and love does not exist apart from discipline and correction. The Bible tells us that everyone whom the Lord loves, he corrects. I've found that God often uses a man's wife to point out areas in relationships he needs to grow in—correction that can actually help him to love his family and even God in a deeper, more meaningful way.

Although a man may fear that responding to suggestions from his wife might open the floodgates to her trying to take over the marriage, I have seen just the opposite to be true. When a woman sees her husband's willingness to accept correction—a mark of someone who wants to gain wisdom—she is more willing to follow his leadership in the home because she values him more highly as her respect for him grows.

How Would You Describe the Ideal Wife?

Can you imagine the ecstatic feeling you would have if your wife volunteered the question, "How can I become a better wife?" The honor you would feel would be overwhelming. Of course, it would be absurd to expect this kind of question to come up between most husbands and wives. But just close your eyes for a moment, lean back in your chair, and picture your wife asking you such a question. It would be great, wouldn't it?

If you want your wife to do this for you, first set the example and work on becoming a better husband. Ask her how you can improve as a husband.

You'll give her new hope for gaining the type of marriage she's always wanted. If she sees you are sincere, ultimately she'll become far more responsive to your needs and desires.

Do you want to be the type of husband wives complain about the most? All you need is an arrogant, all-knowing attitude and an unwillingness to admit when you're wrong. That is not the sacrificial leadership we're called to model (Eph. 5:25). Your role as a husband should follow the model of Jesus Christ. He laid down his life for the church. I am called to lay down my life for Norma. Is your marriage modeling the gospel of Jesus Christ?

Three words produced such disgust in one wife that she said, "I get sick inside and ask myself, 'Why did I ever marry this man? What a mess I have gotten myself into.'" What were those three words he said to her? "I'll never change." According to Scripture, that's a very foolish statement (Prov. 12:15; 18:2). King Solomon taught as long as you have a pulse, there is still hope for you to change (Eccl. 9:4).

"I'll never change," her husband repeated, "so don't try to change me and don't tell me where I need to change. If you think changing is so important, then why don't *you* change and just leave me alone. The biggest change our marriage needs is for you to keep your mouth shut!"

Wives tell me they admire and honor a husband who admits when he is wrong, especially when he openly seeks his wife's advice on how to improve. I believe a man needs to *motivate himself* to become more interested in his wife's ideas on how he can improve (Prov. 9:9). Then when he has asked her advice, he needs to shut up and listen—then follow her advice.

Listen to What She's Really Saying

Here are my three favorite questions for husbands to ask their wives:

1. What kind of marriage would you like to have between 0, really bad, or 10, really great? What would a 10 marriage look like to you?

2. Where are we today on average between 0 and 10? Where have we averaged out in the last year?

3. What would it take for us over the next year to grow closer to the number you would like our marriage to average? Be specific in as many of our marriage areas as you can.

Then, while you are listening to her, look for the meaning behind your wife's statements. It is easier to avoid reacting solely to her words if you actively search for the meaning behind them. Have you ever said to your wife, "You're wrong. I don't *always* do that.

Don't you think you're exaggerating?" She probably didn't mean *always*, as in "every single time." That's just her way to emphasize a point. The *wise* husband looks beyond that offensive word and says, "Tell me how you're feeling right now. Tell me some of the thoughts behind what you just said. Tell me why you feel you need to use the word *always*." Reassure her that she does not have to explain in detail right away. Ask if she'd like to think about it for a day or two. A genuine learner does not put demands on others, forcing them to comply with his impatient desires immediately. He gives others time to feel, think, and change their words.

Many a husband has refused to listen to his wife's correction because of hang-ups over her choice of words. Words have no meaning apart from the interpretation we each place upon them. It is our responsibility in communicating with our wives to understand their *true* intentions.

A husband's tone of voice and facial expressions will reveal whether he has a sincere motivation to learn. His wife will not be as honest if she perceives that he is not really serious about learning and changing.

Chapter 10 delves more into deep communication, so I will conclude with this summary: Avoid reacting to the words your wife uses and look for the meaning or intention behind them.

Let Her Words Sink In

Let your wife's advice sink in like a good spring rain. Hold off on responding until you have deeply received what she has said. Norma told me for years that I frowned when I said certain things to our children. She told me they felt I was angry with them, that I was rejecting them. My furrowed brow frightened them, she said. "I'm not frowning, and I'm not angry," I told her. But after I took the time to look in the mirror, I said, "You're right. I need to work on that. I appreciate you sharing that with me."

Hold Yourself Accountable for Failure

When my children were very young, I used to flick them with my finger on their foreheads or arms when they misbehaved. If one of them was chewing food with his mouth open, I would reach across the table and flick him or her on the head and say, "Cut that out." Norma has made me aware of how this belittles and wounds our children. What a degrading action! Besides, it must hurt. It even hurts my finger.

I knew deep inside that flicking them was not right. Sometimes, right when I did it, Norma would ask, "Kari, how does that make you feel?"

Kari replied, "It always makes me feel bad when Dad does it."

I finally came up with a way to break myself of this habit. I said to each of the children, "If I flick you on the head in anger or irritation, then I will pay you a dollar for each time I do it." (I thought this might work well because I don't like to give money away.) Believe me, my kids were alert enough not to let anything slip by. And I was quickly cured of my flicking habit.

Eventually, you can sometimes even laugh together about something that used to be a problem. On one occasion my son Greg came into the house eating a delicious-looking chocolate candy bar he had just bought. I asked him for a bite. Then Kari and Michael came in and wanted a bite too. Greg soon wished he hadn't unwrapped his candy in front of us. Little Michael didn't think Greg was too generous with the portions he doled out, so he decided to buy his own. He asked Greg where he bought it and how much it cost. Then with a longing look in his eyes, he said, "Dad, would you please flick me? I need a dollar."

Seek Her Forgiveness

As I said before, a woman won't set herself up to be hurt. If you have offended her in the past, she won't be eager to share advice or correction in the present. Seek her forgiveness to reestablish the spirit of communication. Her admiration and respect for you will be strengthened and maintained by your willingness to admit your wrongs. Since chapter 5 dealt with forgiveness, review it from time to time when you need more help in this area.

Receive Her Advice with Gratefulness

Oh, the bounty of a grateful man — less nagging, more admiration and gentleness from his wife. When a man shows genuine gratefulness for his wife's correction, she feels a greater freedom to be more gentle the next time she corrects him. No need to nag when you have a grateful listener. A wife also admires her husband more when he is willing to thank her for her advice or correction. (The only exception is when a wife has been *deeply* hurt by her husband. Then she needs his time and patience until she is able to respond with admiration and gentleness. Don't quit trying when you're so close to success.)

Continue to look for the meaning behind what your wife says, let it sink in, and establish consequences for your failure. When you continue to thank her for helping you, you will begin to see the development of a stronger relationship.

A Final Example

Though the following illustration is the story of a father and son, it can be applied to a husband and wife. Jim's dad was irresponsible in many ways during his son's formative childhood and teen years. He disciplined Jim by kicking him, ridiculing him, scolding him, and slapping him. As a result, his son withdrew in spirit and, consequently, his mind and emotions also withdrew. He moved out of the house. When I explained to this father how he had crushed his son in the past, he realized he had not only damaged their relationship but possibly his son's future relationships.

Because he really wanted to have his son back emotionally, mentally, and physically, this father made an appointment to see his son. It took a lot of nerve, but he admitted to Jim that he was wrong and was sorry for not being the kind of father he should have been. During his confession, he mentioned all the hurtful incidents he could recall.

His son remembered these specific incidents too. "But, Dad, that's not all." Then for the next few minutes he reminded his father of all the other things he had done to hurt him. Jim's father was amazed that his son still remembered it all so vividly. But he begged his son's forgiveness, and they wiped the slate clean. For the first time, Jim reached out to hug his dad.

When you offend your wife, she withdraws mentally, emotionally, and physically. But you can learn to draw her back. Just your willingness to learn will encourage her to respond as she becomes secure in the knowledge that you really want to change.

For Personal Reflection

1. How can a husband become a wise man and increase his love for his wife? See Proverbs 9:8 – 9.

2. What are the consequences of not listening to God's reproofs? See Proverbs 1:22 – 33.

8

IF YOUR WIFE'S
NOT PROTECTED,
YOU GET NEGLECTED

■ ■ ■

*For no one ever hated his own flesh, but nourishes and
cherishes it, just as Christ also does the church.*

Ephesians 5:29

Dan and Janet had been married more than twenty years when he
called me in a panic. "Janet's leaving me for another man," he said.
He was crushed and bewildered. "Gary, is there anything you can do
to help me?"

Dan's main problem was easily detectable when we met to talk.
Let me explain why he lost her by using his hobby as an illustration.

Dan was an avid, meticulous, and knowledgeable gardener. Lush
flower gardens defined the borders of his well-kept yard. Pruned

trees shaded the delicate greenery from the hot summer sun. Dan knew where to plant each variety of flower so it would obtain the proper sunlight and soil. Since each plant had special needs, Dan had taken the time to research those needs so he would know exactly how much fertilizer and other nutrients they required. The results were magnificent. But while his garden was a glorious blaze of harmony in nature, his marriage was wilting from lack of attention. He entered his work and other activities with the same enthusiasm he applied to gardening, which left little time for Janet.

Dan hadn't the faintest idea what Janet's needs were. He had very little knowledge about how to protect her from the "scorching summer sun and wind." Not only did he fail to protect her, but he convinced her through his logical arguments that she should handle household responsibilities that she had said were too much for her. Throughout their twenty years together Dan had failed to listen to her many, many pleadings for tender protection.

Janet was not only holding down a full-time job, but was also responsible for keeping the finances, cooking the meals, cleaning the house, and training the children. She faced many crises alone while Dan was fishing, hunting, or cultivating his posies. He could not recognize Janet's need to have a strong and gentle man to support her during times of stress, one who would protect her from some of the "dirty work" (we all need protection like this at times). She needed to be accepted and loved as a person with her own special physical limitations. When Dan repeatedly failed her, she looked elsewhere.

When a man doesn't understand his wife's limitations or explains them away as laziness, numerous misunderstandings can result. For example, a woman with several small children can be totally exhausted both physically and mentally by five in the evening. If her husband doesn't recognize this, he may resent her avoidance of sexual relations at ten or eleven at night when she is genuinely too tired to even think of a romantic experience with him.

Will They Take Advantage?

Some men think that their wives will take advantage of them if they are gentle, loving, and giving. Keith was willing to gamble money to see if his wife would take advantage of him. He took his wife to a shopping center for her birthday. He told her he would like to help her buy some clothes but never mentioned the amount she could spend. Two hours and ten shops later, as his feet began to ache, Keith wondered whether this birthday outing was a good idea or not.

"Mary, how do you like this dress? It would look good on you."

"No, I don't like it."

Finally they wandered into a nice shop where Mary found a coordinating skirt, jacket, blouse, and suit that she liked well enough to buy. Though the money was beginning to add up, Keith said, "Mary, look at this. Here's a dress on sale."

Mary liked the dress and tried it on.

Keith said, "Why don't you get it?"

"Keith, I shouldn't be spending any more of our money."

"Oh, no, go ahead and get it," Keith replied. "I like it. Hey, Mary, what do you think of this dress?"

"This is getting ridiculous," Mary protested. But she tried it on when Keith insisted.

At this point, he was beginning to wonder if she would buy any of the dresses he told her to buy. "Oh, I like this one, Mary."

"Keith, I cannot buy another dress," she said. "This is getting ridiculous. We can't afford all this."

"Ah, what difference does it make?" he asked. "You're more important than money, and even if I have to work extra, I'm happy to do it." He really put the pressure on her to buy the dress.

She replied, "I'm embarrassed. I can't buy another dress. Please let's pay for these and go get something to eat."

"Come on, Mary. Would you buy just one more for me? I just want this to be a very special day for you!"

"Keith, I can't do it," she said.

"Okay, we'll pay for them. I want you to be happy and satisfied."

Keith didn't admit until sometime later that he just wanted to prove that a woman well-treated will not take advantage. Proud of her willingness to work with him for the financial security they both desired, he praised her for her thriftiness and caution. Now he never worries that Mary will overspend because he knows she will look for the right price and the best buy. Like Norma says, "If it's not on sale, it's not on sale." This experience has also convinced him that Mary will not take advantage of him in other areas of their life.

I'm not advocating that you try this with your wife or in any way test or manipulate her. However, I have often seen what happens when a husband learns what Keith learned: When a wife is treated with tenderness and genuine love, she won't take advantage of the situation. Norma has proven the same truth to me on countless occasions. In fact, she is far more concerned about saving money on each purchase than I will ever be. I love watching Norma bloom as a person. She can buy the best, sharpest-looking clothes for almost nothing. She keeps a record of when certain outfits will be on sale. I so enjoy hearing her say things like, "Do you know how much this cost?"

"Two hundred?" I guess.

"No, I picked it up today for sixteen dollars."

"No way!" I say in genuine disbelief.

When the Scripture teaches that a husband is to cherish his wife (Eph. 5:29), it basically means to protect her, especially in the areas that cause her emotional or physical discomfort.

Discover Where Your Wife Needs Protection

A husband needs to discover areas in which his wife feels vulnerable. Through informal discussions and observation on your part, you can compile mental lists of the major and minor areas where she is frustrated or fearful. For example, driving a car is one of my wife's vulnerable areas. Because she was involved in a serious auto accident in which some good friends were killed, she is naturally very alert to any possible danger when she is driving or even riding in a car. It would only frustrate her if I did not give her the freedom to be cautious, knowing her past circumstances.

She also feels vulnerable when driving long distances alone in the winter because she fears the car will break down. When we lived in Chicago, the car broke down twice, and she had to accept help from passing motorists. Both she and the children could conceivably have been hurt or abused. Since I am aware of her fear, I don't push her to drive long distances alone.

There are many areas where wives may need special consideration and protection from their husbands. Here are just a few examples to get you started thinking.

Consider Her Physical Limitations

Many times a man treats his wife too roughly. He is unaware that his wife's physical makeup may keep her from enjoying roughness even when being playful.

One wife told me that her husband enjoyed wrestling but didn't realize how much it had injured her in the past. He never intentionally hurt her, but she would find bruises on her arms or her body after they had wrestled on the carpet. He was rough with her in other ways too. For example, one night they were in the grocery store, and she lingered a while in the book section. Her husband was waiting for her in the parking lot with a sack of dog food and other items. When she caught up with him, he said, "No wonder you didn't hurry out here. You're not the one holding all the groceries."

"Well, all right, I'll help you," she said. He playfully threw the sack of dog food at her, hitting her in the stomach so forcefully that it left her gasping for breath. The ride home was silent. As they pulled up in the driveway, he said, "The reason I was quiet wasn't because I was mad at you. I was mad at myself for hurting you again." He wanted to make an effort to change his behavior because he realized she needed to be treated with more tenderness and more carefulness.

Relieve Her from Financial Pressures

A man also needs to protect his wife from unnecessary financial stress. Many wives endure a tremendous amount of pressure because of a husband's irresponsibility with finances. To compensate for over-spending, a husband may force his mate to work when she would rather be home with the children. In fact, some husbands demand it, feeling "she should do her part." If a woman is home all day, her husband may expect her to handle online bill payments or balancing the checkbook for the family because he wonders what she does all day anyway. He might think, "I work eight hours every day. The least she can do is pay the bills."

If it were just a matter of bookkeeping, this would not be a problem. But when it comes to facing angry bill collectors, juggling figures in a checkbook that won't balance, coping with mounting pressures resulting from insufficient funds, deciding which bill to pay first, and making phone calls to appease businesses, the burden can become physically and emotionally too much for some wives. The problem is magnified if the husband appears to be spending money loosely and enjoying himself too much.

I made this mistake in the early years of our marriage. Norma worked for a bank, and I logically concluded that anyone working for a bank would obviously be able to take care of the money at home. Since financial matters were a weak point for me at that time, I asked her if she would take that responsibility, which she graciously did for four or five years. One day, though, she came to me in tears, laid the records, the checkbook, and all the bills in my lap and said that she just couldn't handle it anymore. You see, we had two checkbooks between us and only one checking account. I would write a check, hoping the money was in the bank. It was a tremendous pressure on my wife. Today I am very grateful she handed over that responsibility, because it forced me to take more responsibility for the financial well-being of our family. I did the bills and family accounting for fifteen years before she took it back over because I had finally earned a good reputation. But I must confess, I did enjoy it and missed the Saturday mornings with bills.

Take on Household Duties

So many men treat their wives as objects to be used. They don't verbalize it, but they maintain the inward conviction that women should remain in the kitchen cooking or cleaning while they play golf, hunt, or watch the game on TV. Have you ever noticed during get-togethers with friends or relatives that the women are usually the ones who are expected to work in the kitchen while the men just shoot the breeze?

I had a real problem with role expectation during our first few years of marriage: It was Norma's job to cook and my responsibility to fix the car. I finally realized that it was okay for me to cook and clean the house, especially if Norma needed a rest or some time alone away from all of us. We as men need to take a close look at traditional roles and choose what is best based on genuine love and the commitment to cherish our mates. Lately I've taken on more household chores, and Norma loves coming home from work to a clean house. It's like handing her an energy-boosting pill as she walks in.

Think of your wife's special limitations before expecting her to take on added responsibilities. Such forethought will avoid extra strain on your relationship and protect your wife's mental, spiritual, emotional, and physical life.

Let Her Get the Sleep She Needs

Why is it that some men feel their wives need less sleep than they do? While the husband sleeps, the wife prepares breakfast and takes care of the children. This is certainly true where babies are involved. During our early years of marriage, when my children would cry during the night, I automatically expected my wife to get up and take care of them. And she did. Never did I feel compelled to get up and take care of the kids. Be tender and alert to her physical needs. Be the leader in taking whatever steps are needed to ensure that your wife gets the rest she needs.

One of my very worst blunders happened with our first child, Kari. When Kari was about nine months old, Norma got up out of bed around 5:00 a.m. to see why she was crying. Norma left the bedroom door open and I could hear Kari screaming. It irritated me that she had not closed the door. I was in graduate school with tons of after-school studies. So, I yelled at her to please close the door. Kari was keeping me awake. Then it hit me. Not only did I not get up to help Kari, I was complaining about my sweet, loving wife not closing the door. I jumped out of bed and apologized to both and held Kari while Norma returned to our bed.

Take Charge of the Children

My wife often said how much she appreciated the times I took charge of the kids when I came home from work. I got them out from underfoot so she was able to finish dinner peacefully. She was also grateful for the time to be alone. She liked me to take them outside to play, into another room to read, or just to talk to them about whatever topic they chose. After the meal, the children and I often cleared the table and washed the dishes to let Norma have some time off. Instead of resenting her need for my help as I once did, I now look forward to helping her as often as I can.

Thoughtful, creative ideas on your part are worth much more

than the time or energy they cost. They strengthen your marriage and lift your wife's spirit.

One night Jim thrilled Debbie when he asked her to let him cook dinner, set the table, and feed the children. He told her he had a gift he would give her if she let him do those things—a bottle of bath oil. While she took a leisurely bath, he took care of the household chores. It was only a small gift; it just took a bit of Jim's time. But to Debbie, it meant that he understood and cared enough to give something extra of himself.

Limit Your Moves

A move from one city to another is a major step for a woman and requires that her husband be extra sensitive to her. Many times a woman's emotional and physical endurance is depleted just from normal day-to-day routines. A move obviously adds additional stress, even when the move is welcomed. Most women are emotionally connected and deeply related to others after living in a town for a few years. When a husband announces or requests a move, it's not uncommon for the wife to begin crying and showing resistance. Why? She instantly thinks of how painful it will be to leave her friends. And if close relatives are involved, her loss is compounded.

Take Special Care during Stressful Times

We as husbands need to be aware of the amount of stress our wives face daily. To aid your wife with stress, you must first be aware of the situations that are difficult for anyone to handle; these stresses are common to men and women alike. To help you, we have included a list from the Holmes-Rahe Stress Test, which ranks items from the greatest amount of stress to the least amount of stress. The higher it is on the list, the greater the stress it produces. Check to see how much stress you and your wife are facing today.

Holmes-Rahe Stress Test

In the past twelve months, which of these events have happened to you?

Death of a spouse:	100
Divorce:	73
Marital separation:	65
Jail term:	63
Death of a close family member:	63
Personal injury or illness:	53
Marriage:	50
Fired from work:	47
Marital reconciliation:	45
Retirement:	45
Change in family member's health:	44
Pregnancy:	40
Sex difficulties:	39
Addition to family:	39
Business readjustment:	39
Change in financial status:	38
Death of a close friend:	37
Change in number of marital arguments:	35
Mortgage or loan over $10,000:	31
Foreclosure of mortgage or loan:	30
Change in work responsibilities:	29
Son or daughter leaving home:	29
Trouble with in-laws:	29
Outstanding personal achievement:	28
Spouse begins or starts work:	26
Starting or finishing school:	26
Change in living conditions:	25
Revision of personal habits:	24
Trouble with boss:	23
Change in work hours, conditions:	20
Change in residence:	20
Change in schools:	20

Change in recreational habits:	19	
Change in church activities:	19	
Change in social activities:	18	
Mortgage or loan under $10,000:	18	
Change in sleeping habits:	16	
Change in number of family gatherings:	15	
Change in eating habits:	15	
Christmas season:	13	
Vacation:	12	
Minor violation of the law:	11	
TOTAL:		

If your score is 150 or less, there is a 33 percent chance that you will be in the hospital within two years. If it is 150–300, the chances are 51 percent; and 300 and above, 80 percent.

Vow to protect your wife in all areas where she feels fearful or vulnerable, offer help with daily stresses, and show special care during extremely stressful times. That's the first way to show her how much you cherish her.

Discover How Your Wife Wants to Be Fulfilled

Another way to cherish your wife is to help her become fulfilled as a person. You can do this by discovering her personal goals in life and helping her reach them if possible. We all love to know that someone is pulling for us, that others are cheering when we reach a goal. It makes a woman feel worthwhile and valuable when her husband takes time to help her achieve a personal goal.

From time to time, my wife and I get together for a date, for breakfast out, or just for a retreat from home. During that time we list our personal goals. We commit ourselves to help each other fulfill those goals. We actually sit down together and ask each other this question: "For the next twelve months, what would you like to see happen so that you could say, 'Wow, what a great year'?"

This book is the result of a goal that my wife and I wanted to reach together. Since she was as excited about it as I was, I knew it was okay with her for me to take several weeks away from my family to work on our goal. I feel so satisfied, knowing my wife is committed enough to sacrifice for my goals, that I get excited when I think of helping her with her goals. Since I knew she wanted to maintain her physical health as best she could, we decided she should join a health club. To see that she had the opportunity to exercise regularly, I was happy to come home early from work to be with the kids so she could accomplish her personal goal of good physical health.

Sit down with your wife and ask her to name some goals. She might want to go back to school, advance in her vocation, study public speaking, learn to sew, or cook some new exotic meals. Her goals may change as she discovers the real pressure or motives behind them. Maybe she says she wants to go back to school, when all she really wants is a couple of days a week away from the children. By relieving her of some of the pressure, you may help channel her energies in the right direction, helping her to reach her *real* personal goals. I believe it is our responsibility to discover our wives' goals and to understand how they want to fulfill themselves as women. Then we must let them be who they want to be by respecting their unique ambitions.

Be extra careful that you don't torpedo her ambitions. At one time my wife wanted to share with women how to be fulfilled in the home without outside work. Unfortunately, during our early marriage she became timid when speaking to groups, because I used to correct her grammar or give suggestions on how to improve her teaching methods in an insensitive way. Eventually she stopped speaking in front of groups because of my criticism. It took five years of my praise and encouragement to heal the wounds I had thoughtlessly inflicted. She is speaking to groups more and more now, but she is still quite nervous when I am in the audience.

Has your wife ever told you emphatically in the morning that she is going to lose weight … and that very same evening she's eating donuts? The harmful action you can take is to remind her sarcastically of that early-morning commitment. However, you can comfort her by saying nothing at all or by putting your arm around her to say, "I love you for who you are, not for what you decide to do." She probably feels disappointed enough about her lack of willpower. Knowing she is loved *as she is* will probably boost her self-confidence and strengthen her willpower.

Pinpoint Her Needs

In summary, a woman loves to build a lasting relationship with a man who cares about her enough to let her lean on him when she needs comfort. She needs a man who will understand her fears and limitations so that he can protect her. She feels important when her husband stands up and defends her in the presence of someone who is criticizing her.

Each person is unique, and the only way you can pinpoint your wife's needs is to discuss them with her. You may want to question her to see if she feels that you are protective or helpful enough in these areas:

- The family finances and budgets
- Raising the children
- Household duties and responsibilities
- The future—insurance, a will, retirement investments
- Her job and/or volunteer commitments
- Her friends and relatives

You should also endeavor to discover how she would like to be fulfilled as a person. Ask her to explain two or three goals she has always wanted to accomplish. Then reevaluate your goals together each year and look for ways to meet them. Ultimately, two happy and fulfilled people make for a happy and fulfilling marriage.

For Personal Reflection

1. Clearly define the word *cherish* as it is used in Ephesians 5:29. Ask your pastor for help or consult a Bible commentary.

2. How does Paul encourage Christians to treat each other? How do you treat your wife (1 Thessalonians 5:11, 14)?

9

ARGUMENTS . . . THERE'S A BETTER WAY

■ ■ ■

For this reason a man shall leave his father
and mother and shall be joined to his wife
and the two shall become one flesh.

Ephesians 5:31

A simple agreement can eliminate heated arguments between you and your wife. No, it's not a divorce!

It is an agreement that will increase the time you and your mate spend discussing important areas *without* that familiar anger and silence routine; it will also build your wife's self-respect.

When my wife and I stumbled upon this concept during a Fourth of July argument several years ago, both of our fuses were getting short. The fireworks show was dull in comparison. I wanted to vacation in Colorado in July; she wanted to go to Florida in August. Since we didn't agree on separate vacations either, the discussion became hotter and hotter with no end in sight. Sizzling, I compared her attitude to some of the more submissive single women from the office.

"You don't have a calm attitude. Besides that, you're wrong," I said.

"I have never met this 'calm woman' you talk about," she replied angrily. "If you can show me just one, I might consider following her example."

At this point, the accidental brainstorm that has helped us avoid heated discussions for several years came to me. I asked Norma if she would be willing to drop the conversation and try an experiment for just two months. If it worked, we'd use it; if not, we'd search for another solution.

"Will you not make decisions in the home that affect me and the rest of the family without my complete agreement?" I asked her. "And I won't make any decisions affecting you unless I have your full consent."

I didn't know if the experiment would work, but I did know that I was tired of arguments and futile discussions that led nowhere except to tears and angry silence. Since I worked for an organization that taught family harmony, I was desperate to achieve it in my own home. (You've heard of the plumber with leaky pipes, haven't you?)

Many things had to change if we were going to agree to agree. We had to reason together for longer periods of time. We were also forced to discover the reasons behind each other's comments. I had to search for the meaning behind Norma's words and understand her frame of reference if I hoped to convince her of my point of view. Several of our first discussions ended with the consensus that since we couldn't agree we would just wait. Amazingly enough, many "problems" seemed to solve themselves—or at least their importance seemed to diminish as the days passed.

In spite of the success of our agreement, I went back on it after two months. Hearing a growing argument between Kari and Greg at the kitchen table, I rushed in to referee just in time to see Greg shove his full plate across the table, spilling it all over Kari. I was about to take Greg upstairs for a little discipline when Norma said she disagreed.

"Well, our experiment doesn't apply in every situation," I argued. "I can't relinquish my responsibility as Greg's father just because you don't agree. I'm sorry. I'll have to overrule you this time."

After Greg and I had our little talk, Norma greeted me coldly in the kitchen.

"Well, Norma, I had to do what I thought was right," I explained. "I wish we could agree in every situation, but it's not practical."

She replied, "I don't think you took the time to find out the facts."

"I saw all I needed to know."

But I had to admit that I didn't know what Kari had done to provoke Greg. Norma had told Kari to make sandwiches for Greg. Kari probably didn't want to do it in the first place, so when Greg didn't want the sandwiches, she tried to force them on him.

"Mom told me to make you sandwiches and you're gonna eat 'em," she said.

"You're not my boss. I don't have to eat them," Greg retorted. And to make his point, he pushed the sandwiches away. But the table was slicker than he anticipated, and the sandwiches slid into Kari's lap.

I admitted to Greg that I was wrong and apologized. To keep such mistakes from happening in the future we obtain all the legal counsel needed from within the family. After all the facts are presented, the family decides who is guilty. We also set up written contracts covering desired behaviors, and these were of tremendous help during our children's teenage years. (See my book *The Key to Your Child's Heart* for details of this powerful parenting method.)

Whenever Norma and I do not agree on something that affects

the family, I have been amazed at the number of times her decision has been right. I'm not sure whether she has a hotline to heaven or what, but somehow she can sense when something is not right. Committing ourselves to agree has brought more harmony and deeper communication than anything else we practice. It has increased my wife's self-worth and eliminated pressure-packed arguments.

Constant disagreement can only weaken a marriage relationship. That's probably why Paul emphasized having oneness of spirit and mind in the church. He likened the struggle for oneness to an athlete *striving* to reach the goal (Phil. 1:27). Likewise, as husbands and wives we can learn to enter into oneness or agreement.

As I mentioned earlier, I know some men will react strongly to having their wives share in any of the decisions that affect the family. Like battlefield generals, they demand acceptance of their orders, not input from those people the decisions will most affect.

As we'll discuss at the end of the chapter, there may be rare times of deadlock when you'll have to make the final decision that goes against your wife's or your family's feelings. However, I've found that by my slowing down, talking through major decisions with Norma and the children, and valuing their opinions and input, over the years such impassable situations have been almost nonexistent.

The rest of this chapter discusses the specific consequences of not agreeing on decisions that affect the family and ways to apply the agreement principle in your family.

What Happens When You Make All the Decisions

When a wife is left out of the decision-making process, she feels insecure and unsafe, especially if the decisions involve financial security or living conditions. Her constant state of insecurity spreads like a disease to produce instability in other areas of the marriage. But before you choose to blame your wife for the mistakes and failures that come your way, you might want to consider that God has difficulty blessing those who are not joined in unity. Take the following stories as examples of what can happen when *you* make all the decisions.

Business Failure

Steve and Bonney had been struggling to make just enough money to put food on the table. His small business was requiring eighteen hours a day on his part, and she was putting in at least eight hours a day at the office, even though she was seven months pregnant. Steve flew east to show his business ideas to a multimillionaire. The man was impressed and made Steve a generous offer, which he accepted in less than five minutes. It seemed the only reasonable course of action.

He could hardly wait to call Bonney and tell her the great news in logical order so she could get as excited as he was. He told her, "First, you won't have to work anymore. Second, he's giving me 20 percent of the profits—he says I'll be a millionaire in a year. Third, you won't believe how beautiful it is back here, and he's going to pay all of the moving expenses."

Steve was shocked to hear uncontrollable weeping on the other end of the line. At first he thought she was crying for joy. (I know it's hard to believe, but he actually thought that.)

As soon as Bonney caught a breath, she had a chance to ask some questions Steve considered totally ridiculous (in fact, he thought her mind had snapped). She asked questions like, "What about our parents?" and, "What about our apartment—I just finished the room for the baby." With her third question, Steve, in all of his masculine sensitivity, abruptly terminated the phone call. She had the nerve to ask if he'd forgotten she was seven months pregnant!

After giving her an hour or two to pull herself together, he called her back. She had gained her composure and agreed to move back east. She left her parents, her friends, her doctor and childbirth classes, and the nursery she had spent so much time preparing for her first child.

It took Bonney almost eight months to adjust to a change that

Steve had adjusted to in minutes. Steve never made his million. The business failed eight days before their baby was born, and they moved again. Steve eventually learned his lesson, and today he doesn't make any major change unless Bonney is in agreement. He tries to give her ample time to adjust to other changes as soon as he can foresee them. However, Steve will never forget the loving sacrifices his wife made so many times. He even realizes that questions like "What about our parents?" or, "What about the nursery?" can be more meaningful than money.

Financial Losses

Husbands can make their wives feel stupid, inadequate, or like an unnecessary member of the family when they make most of the decisions alone. Many husbands treat their wives as if they don't know anything at all. When a decision comes up in their area of expertise or with regard to financial dealings, their wives might as well forget about participating as far as they are concerned.

Jerry had to lose money before he would respect his wife's judgment. He considered a number of ways to invest some of his earnings, from apartments, to real estate, to the stock market. After talking to developers and reading literature, he decided to buy a lake-front lot in a planned retirement community. He reasoned that if he bought the land during the early development stages, it would be worth quite a bit of money in five to ten years. When Linda found out about his plans, she hesitated to invest their money.

But Jerry thought, "What would she know anyway?" and signed the contract in spite of her objections.

Sometime later when he wanted to sell the land for quick money to invest in a better project, he found it was difficult to sell. Jerry and Linda will probably still have it when they are ready to retire. If Jerry had consulted Linda, not only would he have saved a great deal of money, but he could have given her self-esteem a boost. After all, what's wrong with becoming "one flesh" with our mates? That's God's design!

Physical Collapse

We husbands would do well to remember that everyone has a different stress-tolerance level. When you ignore your wife in making decisions, you add stress to every area of her life. As I've said before, stress will definitely take its toll by eroding her physical health.

As with so many areas of my marriage, I had to discover this the hard way. As I mentioned earlier, when my work load demanded that I travel a great deal, I didn't ask Norma if she could handle three small children alone; I just assumed she could. As a result of the extra pressure, she came to me on the verge of a physical collapse. I had to take a less responsible position in my company, but I learned the importance of taking care of my family.

Family Strife

When you make all decisions without regard to the welfare of your family, you are sure to reap grief and regret. I look back on the past with horror when I think of incidents like the following: Norma and the three children were to pick me up at work at 5:00 p.m. to go for hamburgers. Just as she drove up, I was called to a last-minute staff meeting. I explained quickly that I would join her in a few minutes. Instead, the meeting lasted two hours. She waited for me, but was understandably out of patience by the time the meeting was over. Instead of telling my boss that my family was waiting, I stayed in an unnecessary meeting for two hours. To make matters worse, I wasn't apologetic when I got down to the car. I was angry because Norma had not waited lovingly and patiently for me while appeasing our three hungry children.

If only I could relive that experience! I would say, "Honey, they just called an unexpected meeting. Would you like to go ahead without me and feed these hungry kids? Just bring me back a burger and I'll eat it later." Or I would explain to my associates that I had a previous commitment to my family. Let's face it, not much is usually accomplished at meetings held that late in the day. (And your colleagues' families might benefit from it too.)

Arguments and Verbal Attacks

Finally, arguments are probably the most common side effects of major decisions made apart from any discussion. As anger sharpens the tongue, turning it into a fierce weapon, husbands and wives can end discussions by attacking each other's character. Words spoken during the heat of an argument are sometimes never forgotten. My wife can still remember ugly things I said when we were dating.

If a woman feels threatened during a discussion, she may become angry and demand her way. If her husband doesn't understand that she is acting that way because he threatened her security, he may feel his ego is being attacked or his leadership questioned. And both will pursue the issue like wild dogs, fighting to be the leader of the pack.

The No-Loser Policy

Today, my wife and I employ the no-loser policy. It's just not acceptable to either of us for our mate to feel like a loser in any solution to a mutual disagreement. We actually take the time to highly honor each other by listening to both sides, accounting for both our needs and our feelings. Then together, we both try to come up with a solution that we both love. This works like magic. After we achieve understanding, a solution usually appears to one of us in time. The key again is *understanding* the feelings and needs of your mate.

Suppose a husband who is having difficulties with his wife comes up with the idea of the two of them taking a short vacation for a few days to better their relationship, while leaving the kids with grandma. His wife may say, "You're pressuring me." He feels he has been verbally slapped in the face. He wasn't trying to pressure her, and furthermore, he sees no logical reason why she should feel that way. Tempers flare, and argument number 1,241 begins. But who's counting? The point is, if a woman says she feels pressured, take her word for it—she feels pressured! Try to enter her world to discover why she feels that way — don't argue that you didn't intentionally try to pressure her. If your idea somehow has caused her to say she *feels* pressured, then she *is* pressured.

The chart below gives an example of how to eliminate trivial arguments before they snowball into major flare-ups.

If she says ...	Typical response from a husband	Try this instead ...
"You're putting pressure on me."	"I'm not pressuring you. I just wanted to do something so the two of us could be together. Don't accuse me of that."	"Honey, I can sure understand that you're pressured. If you feel what I'm saying is pressuring you, then I can sure accept that. That's not my intent, but I can understand that you feel that way. Can you share at this time any of the reasons why you feel that way?"
"I hate going to the beach. I don't want to go."	"You used to like the beach before we were married."	"I know I should know why you don't want to go to the beach, but could you tell me just once more some of the reasons why you don't?"*

*She may have several reasons for saying this, one being that she is embarrassed about her figure. At that point a husband needs to be tender, understanding, and gentle. Remember, some women do not feel as relaxed in a bathing suit as a man might.

If she says ...	Typical response from a husband	Try this instead ...
"I don't want to go to the game with you. They're boring."	"I try to do things with you. The least you could do is to go with me once in a while and support me in something that I enjoy doing."	"Honey, is one of the reasons that you don't like to go because I ignore you so much when I'm at a ball game?"**

How to Make Decisions Together

Once you have found a method that works, stick to it. Whenever my wife and I try to take shortcuts, we get into trouble.

After a quick discussion about moving to the country, we located the home of our dreams. I wrote an ad for the paper to sell our home and bought "For Sale" signs to put in the front yard. A neighbor walked across the street to ask how much I was asking for our house. When I quoted the price, he said it was far too low; it might reduce the market value of other houses in the neighborhood.

A vague uneasiness began to gnaw at me. Since Norma and I had not discussed every detail of this upcoming move, I tried to call her but couldn't reach her. I cancelled the ad and plucked the signs out of the yard. When Norma finally arrived home, we filled out the chart we usually use for major decisions and decided, after weighing advantages and disadvantages, that it was not a good idea for us to sell our home at that time.

The simple chart we use helps us reach total agreement on

**If she says yes to that question, ask her for other reasons she resists going to a game. (Remember, if you react negatively to her reasons, she'll be less willing to share her true feelings with you in the future.) You may need to give her room to breathe and come back to it another time. If she says no, ask her to explain why, tenderly and with a real desire to understand her and value her opinion.

important decisions. We first list all of the reasons, pro and con, for doing something. Second, we list all the reasons, pro and con, for not doing it. Third, we evaluate each reason. Will the decision have lasting effects? Is the reason selfish or will it help others? Finally, we total the pros and cons and see which wins, not *who* wins. Although you may think you have in mind all the reasons you need to make the decision, seeing them ranked in black and white simplifies and streamlines the decision.

The pro-and-con chart forces us as a couple to consider as many facts as possible. For instance, if I am counseling someone, I find I usually cannot help the person until I know plenty of facts about the particular situation. The fewer the facts, the foggier a situation appears. But the more facts I have, the clearer the picture and the easier the solution. If I ask a person to write down all the facts on a piece of paper, often he or she can come up with the solution on his or her own.

Let me give you an example of how the chart worked for my family.

A Major Decision — Should I Change Jobs?

This job change would mean moving a thousand miles and would involve a cut in pay.

1. List all the reasons, pro and con, for changing jobs and moving my family a thousand miles. (I'll only put down a few of the reasons we used, for purposes of illustration.)

If We Move

What we will gain (pro)	*What we will lose (con)*
1. We will be able to raise our family in a smaller town.	1. We will be taking a cut in pay. Could we adjust to that?

What we will gain (pro)	*What we will lose (con)*
2. We will gain a greater opportunity to help families in a concentrated way.	2. Do we really want to live in a small town and lose all the conveniences of a major city with nice shopping centers?
3. There are many more camping spots where we're moving, and the weather is warmer year-round.	3. We'll have to move away from our friends whom we love so much.
4. Two of our best friends live in that town.	4. Can we afford to buy our own home?
	5. There's not a major airport for convenient travel to my family workshops.

2. List all of the reasons, pro and con, for *not* moving my family to a new location and a new job.

If We Stay

What we will gain (pro)	*What we will lose (con)*
1. We will maintain our present salary.	1. We will lose our opportunity to help families on a personal and consistent basis.
2. Our children will be educated at a private school.	2. We will lose the opportunity for our children to live in a warmer climate with a greater opportunity for involvement in sports and activities.
3. We will continue to use all the shops and stores that we know so well.	3. We'll lose our chance to join a church that we as a family really enjoy attending together.

4. We will continue all the contacts we have for buying various items at discount.	4. We will lose our opportunity as husband and wife to work on our life goals together.

It's important to list reasons for *doing* something and *not doing* something. It forces us to think of different aspects of both viewpoints.

3. Evaluate each of the reasons given in both lists. Make your decision based on your evaluations of both lists.

"Vote Yes on the Big Move," Kari's sign read. She had plastered signs all over the house to gain votes in favor of our move to another state. Like a campaign manager, she actively tried to get our other two children to cast their votes for her side.

When voting day came, I passed out a ballot to each family member. The suspense mounted as I read each vote aloud until finally the votes were tallied. "Yes" won unanimously.

The doctrine of majority rule doesn't apply here. If one member had voted "No," I believe it would have been important to consider *why* that member had voted differently. An essential ingredient in making a happy family is total agreement. Discussion should stay open until everyone can agree when possible. Creative alternatives can be considered when it looks as though one member is going to hang the jury.

Deadlock!

What should a couple do if they are deadlocked on an important decision? Instead of looking for a referee for the ensuing battle, they should postpone the decision as long as possible in order to gather additional facts. If it comes down to the wire and they still can't agree, the husband should make his decision with the *family's* best interest in mind. A loving, understanding attitude can melt a wife's heart and give her the security she so desperately wants in times of difficult decisions, even if it takes time to adjust to a decision.

For Personal Reflection

1. Is a husband instructed to submit to his wife (Eph. 5:21)?

2. What do the verses before and after Ephesians 5:22 mean, where a wife is instructed to submit? Also check Colossians 3:17–19.

3. Since a husband is to love his wife as Christ loves the church, it is essential that we know how Christ loves. What can we learn about him from Matthew 20:25–28?

4. Write out a simple definition of submission. Consider Romans 12:10.

A SUCCESSFUL MARRIAGE ... IT'S EASIER THAN YOU THINK

■ ■ ■

"While I was with them, I protected them
and kept them safe by that name you gave me."

John 17:12 NIV

When I was newly married, I often asked other couples if they could tell me the secrets of a happy marriage. They would usually say, "You and your wife will have problems, but if it's meant to be, you'll stay together. If not, you'll separate." Later, when I worried about staying close to my children, people would answer, "Your teenagers will rebel. It's just normal."

These philosophies seemed so pessimistic that I became discouraged whenever our domestic harmony was threatened during an argument. I couldn't find any articles or books written on how to become a warm, loving family.

However, today I can say without reservation that my wife is my best friend. This has come about because we have practiced a principle learned from several successful families. Practicing this principle also has eliminated any significant disharmony in our family and has drawn us all closer.

I learned this principle by interviewing over a hundred couples across the nation. I chose them initially because they seemed to have close relationships with each other and with their children. Although many of the children were teenagers, all seemed to be close to their parents and happy about it. They were enthusiastic families — radiantly happy in most instances.

When I spoke to different groups, I would scan the audience, looking for the family that seemed the happiest. Then I would interview them afterward. I often talked to the wife alone, then the husband, and finally the children. I always asked them the same questions: "What do you believe is the main reason you're all so close and happy as a family?" Without exception, each member of each family gave the same answer: "We do a lot of things together." Even more amazing to me was that all the families had *one particular activity in common.*

I can truthfully say I have tested the suggestions of these families enough to prove they are valid. I no longer fear my family will break up. Nor do I fear my children will reject my wife and me as they grow older. That's because my family is practicing the things those other successful families suggested.

I kept wondering, "Why does sharing activities together draw a marriage and a family into a closer knit and more loving unit?"

Jesus left us an example by sharing his life with the disciples. They traveled, ate, slept, healed, and ministered *together.* He guided, guarded, and kept them; then he prayed for them (John 17). His example of togetherness and oneness constantly inspires me to become one with my family by scheduling many times to be together.

Happy Campers

But there was one activity that every family I interviewed specifically mentioned. They all thought that camping together was the number-one secret to a happy family. I was confused by the answer, but we looked into camping as a possible recreational activity. Norma's first thought was of bugs, snakes, dirt, and all sorts of creepy-crawlies. She didn't like camping. Though I had been camping only a few times, I couldn't remember having any insurmountable problems. We decided to give it a try. Norma reluctantly agreed, frantically clutching a can of insect repellent and stuffing mosquito coils into her purse.

We borrowed a pop-top camper and found a beautiful campsite in Kentucky. Though I was nervous being all alone in the woods, I didn't say anything. After we parked next to the only bright street-light within fifty feet of the showers, we built a campfire to roast hot dogs and marshmallows. It was peaceful. No one was around to distract us. We put the children to bed around nine, and then Norma and I stayed up to enjoy a romantic evening. A distant thunderstorm entertained us with a light show as we enjoyed a warm breeze. Though the lightning came closer and closer, we thought it was passing to one side of us and went to bed with light hearts.

The children were asleep as I crawled into a tiny bed with Greg, and Norma joined Kari. We were lying close enough to touch hands while we whispered softly. I thought, "Boy, this is really the life. I can see why everybody likes to camp." But my feeling of serenity was blasted away as the storm arrived, lashing furiously around us and knocking out the streetlight beside our tent. It was pitch black except for the frequent jagged streaks illuminating the sky. Thunder rumbled, shaking the ground beneath us, and the wind began to howl. Rain beat against our tent until the water forced its way through, soaking our pillows.

"Honey, do you think this camper is going to blow over?" Norma asked faintly.

"No, not a chance," I said. I really thought the camper was going to *blow up*. I knew we were going to die. But within an hour, the storm's wrath cooled enough to let the stars shine through again. We lay there breathlessly on our soaked pillows, each wondering silently whether camping was the life for us. I continued to wonder why camping played such an important part in drawing families together. Of course, any family that faced sure death together and survived would be closer!

Colorado was the destination for our own trip in our own trailer. We could hardly wait to experience the beauty of snow-capped peaks and sniff the aroma of pine trees. I could already hear the sizzle of rainbow trout frying in the pan. As we started up the mountain, our station wagon slowed from fifty miles per hour to thirty, then to twenty-five, then to twenty, until we finally slowed to the pace of fifteen miles per hour. "Hot," read the temperature gauge. I felt like I was wired to the engine because my palms were sweating so. Our children sensed the tension in the air and became hyper and loud.

"I've got to stop at the next pull-off area," I told them. My nerves were frayed as I pulled over. All three kids jumped out immediately. I hadn't even had time to worry about the overheated car when our youngest, Michael, screamed at the top of his lungs.

His older brother, relieving some pent-up energy, had kicked what he thought to be an empty can. Unfortunately, it was half-full of transmission fluid. The can had landed upside down on Michael's head, and he was covered from head to toe, a terribly unhappy little boy. His nose, his ears, even his mouth were dripping with it. Not expecting such a calamity, we had no water in the trailer to clean him up. We worried that he had injured his eyes because he blinked rapidly the rest of the trip.

I've mentioned only the tragic times of our camping experiences, but we've also had tremendous experiences hiking to tops of mountains and exploring the out-of-doors. Camping truly did bring our family together like no other activity could.

Whatever Floats Your Boat

Camping not your thing? Try some other activity—whatever floats your boat. Literally! Many families do enjoy boating together.

Norma called one day to ask if I would like to buy a water-skiing boat and equipment. Though I was unsure at first, the idea seemed to appeal to everyone in the family. We purchased an "extremely experienced" model. When we were bouncing across the lake on our first time out, I noticed my wife holding on to the side as if she feared we would capsize at any moment. I thought I had everything under control, yet panic was clearly written on her face. She gripped the windshield with one hand while the other had a death grip on the bar beside her.

"Norma, what's wrong?" I questioned.

"I hate boats," she said slowly.

"You've got to be kidding. You hate boats? You're the one who called me up and said you wanted to buy the boat, and now you're telling me you hate boats? Would you like to explain that?"

I slowed our speed and let the boat idle so she could relax enough to talk to me.

"All my life I've been afraid of boats," she said. "I've just always had a real problem with boats." I sat there in total bewilderment as she labored to explain that she hated boats, but she knew she could learn to like them. She determined to endure boating long enough to learn to like it for the family's sake, and sure enough, she enjoys it much more now.

Not long after our first boating experience, I sat next to an executive from the Boeing company on a flight to Seattle. When I asked him about his family, he told me they were very close.

"What is the most important thing that holds your family together?" I asked.

"Several years ago," he said, "we purchased a yacht, and as a family we traveled around the various inlets and islands in the Seattle area. My family enjoys boating so much that it has provided a tremendous way to knit us together."

Of course you needn't buy a boat or trailer in order to enjoy family togetherness. Any shared interest or activity can draw a family together. I've known families who walk through community parks, swim at the local recreation center, and have regular family game nights. In an age where people increasingly hide behind their cell phones, computers, or iPods, it's especially important to unplug and find ways to enjoy simply being together, laughing and talking and building memories.

The Importance of Spending Time Together

What happens when you don't spend time together as a family? One man sadly admitted to me that when he and his children meet for a rare get-together they hardly have a thing in common.

"It's a sickening experience," he said, "to have your children back home for a visit and have nothing in common. You know, the only thing we ever laugh about as a family is when we remember the one time we took a three-week vacation. We rented a tent and camped. What a vacation! We still laugh at those experiences."

He didn't have any other fond memories of family togetherness. His wife had her clubs; he had his clubs; the children had their activities. They all grew apart in separate worlds.

"Now that my wife and I are alone, we have very little in common," he lamented. "We are two lonely people lost in our five-bedroom house."

The simple principle of sharing life together permeated every area of our family life, from supporting Greg and Michael in soccer to supporting Kari and Greg in piano. As much as possible, we looked for ways to spend time together—cooking, fishing, putting the kids to bed, gardening. Everything we did as a family assured me of our unity later in life. My kids to this day still talk about our quality time spent as a family. I am very close to all three of my adult children, and I believe our family activities are a major reason why.

Family outings are some of the best ways to share your life together. To plan a successful outing, find out what activities you and your wife and your children would like to do together. Next, consider everyone's schedule to see if the planned outing will force hardship on anyone involved. For example, we agreed as a family that Greg should not be involved in group sports for a time because we felt we should be camping on weekends instead of sitting on bleachers watching him play football. Plan something that will interest and involve each family member in some way. For longer trips, you can balance out activities, perhaps seeing a ballgame one day, and shopping another day. But be sure to include an activity that you *all* can enjoy together.

The importance of spending time together is powerfully illustrated by an experience I had with my daughter. When Kari was nine years old, I sensed an undefined barrier between us. I couldn't detect anything specific. We just weren't close. I didn't enjoy being with her, and she didn't enjoy me either. No matter how hard I tried, I couldn't break through the barrier. From time to time, Norma would comment that I preferred my sons over my daughter. I said, "One of the reasons is because the boys are more responsive to me."

"You'd better do something to strengthen the relationship now," Norma said, "because when Kari gets older it will be much harder." So I tested the value of belonging and decided to take Kari with me on my next seven-day business trip. Though we still weren't close, she became excited as we planned what to do and where to stay. During the plane trip we worked on her multiplication problems until it almost drove me (and the man in front of us) crazy. We stayed with a farm family in Washington the first night. I noticed the rapport Kari and I felt as we laughed and sang around the dinner table with their numerous children; we were actually enjoying one another's company. At times we didn't even talk. It seemed enough just to be together. Kari seemed to have just as much fun in that farm home as she did helping me with my meetings. I let her distribute some of the material so she really felt she was a special part of my team. And she was.

We decided to take the scenic route from Portland to Seattle. I wanted to show her the small "poke and plum" town near Portland where I was raised. It's so small that by the time you "poke" your head out of the window you're "plum" out of the town. After we had a flat tire near the Columbia River, we changed it together and then walked down to the river to gather driftwood for a memento. We tried to make it up a snow-covered mountain, but had to turn around and go all the way back to Seattle the long way. We will both remember that trip, good times and bad.

I have *never* sensed a barrier between us in the years since that trip. I feel complete harmony and oneness in Kari's company. Thirty-four years later, she still has the piece of driftwood from that trip. It's a silent reminder of our bond and her special relationship with Christ—on it is engraved her salvation date.

Let Hard Times Draw You Together

War foxholes make lasting friendships. Haven't you heard the stories of buddies who fought together in the same regiment? Whenever they meet, there is an instant camaraderie that no one can ever take away from them, a feeling born from surviving a struggle together. Trials can produce maturity and loving attitudes (James 1:2–4). All major sports teams have that same closeness because of the "battles" they fought together.

Families have foxholes too. Even when a crisis inflicts deep scars, the dilemma can draw the family closer.

I finally realized that camping is "scheduled disasters." Maybe it's the crises in camping that have such a unifying effect on a family. Any family that can survive bugs, poison ivy, storms, burnt sausage, and sand in the eggs has to come out of the ordeal closer. During a crisis, you have only each other to rely on. We all look back on the mishaps that occurred during our camping trips and laugh, though it wasn't a bit funny at the time.

Like the night Norma awakened me at two in the morning so cold that she asked, "Honey, could you take us home?" Though we were two hours from home, I abandoned my cozy bed to pack and leave. She called me her John Wayne on the way home, but at the time I didn't feel much like the Duke.

Our camping fiascos have been numerous. "Only two more hours and home sweet home," I thought after our first camping trip. Tension electrified the air as we all longed to be home with hot water and familiar beds once again. Now when we look back on the experience we laugh, and our laughter binds us together as husband and wife and as parents and children.

But just as important as family time is time spent together as a couple. Let's turn now to look at how we can build in shared experiences in our marriage relationship beyond times we spend with each other as a family.

Couple Time

When I think of a trip to Hawaii, I envision snorkeling, scuba diving, spear fishing, or anything related to being in the water. My wife thinks of an orchid lei as she steps off the airplane, dining in romantic restaurants, and sightseeing during the day. Our desires are completely different.

Although a husband and wife both need time to enjoy separate activities, they also need to step into the world of their mates to taste each other's interests. While my wife is shopping, I might be snorkeling, but at night we would dine together in a very romantic place. At times my wife would want to snorkel with me, and I would enjoy sightseeing with her. I'm not saying that I would rather be touring than snorkeling or that she would rather slip on a wet suit instead of a new dress, but we believe it is important to compromise in order to share experiences. Afterwards, when the trip is only a hotel receipt in your wallet, it's the experiences you shared during the trip that will draw you together.

I often ask couples if they ever do things together. When I ask about vacations and the husband's face lights up while the wife grimaces, I usually conclude they took their vacation at the husband's chosen site. It was probably a dream to him and sheer torture for her and the children.

As you look at your life, think of activities that you can share together with your wife. Look at your Christian life. How can you share church activities beyond attending worship services together? When and how often will you pray? Is there a Bible study you can attend together? Would you enjoy attending a Christian conference or concert together? How about volunteer opportunities — is there a ministry you would enjoy working on together?

Then take some time to think about and discuss trips or vacations. What would your dream trip be? What would it include? What are two of your favorite activities? What are two of your wife's favorite activities? Could you plan a trip that includes all those activities in one place?

Finally, ask your wife to write down ten activities she enjoys doing. Then ask her to name which activities she'd like to do with you. Don't be surprised if she prefers doing some things alone — or if she doesn't enjoy being with you at all. If she has no desire to share activities with you, reflect on your attitude toward her in the past. Have you been critical or bored? Did you pout when you had to do something she wanted to do? If so, she will remember those times and tend to avoid involvement with you in the future. You will need to show her through your changed attitude and actions that you value spending time with her, even when doing things that only she enjoys.

The One Activity That Wives Enjoy the Most with Their Husbands

Many women have told me about the importance of intimate communication with their husbands — special togetherness times — after the children are in bed, during the day on the phone, at breakfast, at dinner, at a restaurant over a cup of coffee. These special sharing times can be the most enjoyable part of a woman's day or week.

My wife agrees that an intimate sharing time with me is the one thing she enjoys most about our relationship. We make it a point to have breakfast together as often as possible at a nearby restaurant just to talk about our upcoming schedules. I ask her questions about what she needs for the week and what I can do to help her and vice versa. I enjoy our discussions because I know she enjoys them. But more importantly, I would really miss those times of intimate communication if we ever neglected them.

To really understand each other during our conversations, we use a concept seldom taught in the classroom. It's called the "revolving method" of communication. Though it's very simple, you'll find it a tremendous help in avoiding misunderstandings. It involves four steps:

1. I ask my wife to share her feelings or thoughts with me.
2. I respond by rephrasing what I think she said.
3. She answers either yes or no.
4. If she answers no, I continue to rephrase what I think she said until I get a yes response.

My wife goes through the same four steps when I am explaining my feelings to her. Our communication is more meaningful since neither of us assumes that we automatically know what the other is saying. (In the past, misunderstandings over implied meanings confused and ruined many discussions.) This simple process has nearly eliminated misinterpretations in our marriage.

For Personal Reflection

1. How can Paul's example of discipleship in 1 Thessalonians 2:7–11 be applied to a family relationship?

2. Plan out a simple way to become "one flesh" (Eph. 5:31) by sharing an activity with your wife.

11

SO YOU WANT
A PERFECT WIFE

■ ■ ■

*I will not presume to speak of anything except
what Christ has accomplished through me.*

Romans 15:18

Basically, I started off as an uneducated fool in our marriage. Some older husband told me that if you want a great marriage, tell her to follow Scripture and obey you in everything. That sounded good to me, but he left out the next verses in the Bible, "Husbands, lay down your life for your wife" (paraphrased). In my own worldwide interviews with women, I never met one who resisted the idea of submission if the husband was loving, tender, highly valuing her, caring, and willing to listen and deeply communicate with her on an equal level.

Sadly I started at the honeymoon saying stupid things like, "If you were more submissive to me, we wouldn't have near as many problems." And I usually had that holier-than-thou voice. I was sure we would have a harmonious and fulfilling marriage if only I could motivate her to change her attitudes and responses toward me. And I was always thinking of new, creative, foolproof ways to make her change. Of course, my creative ideas usually just made her more resistant, but I didn't let that deter me. After all, most, if not all, our problems were *her* fault, I thought.

I even said things like, "You're so stubborn and strong-willed; you're causing our marriage to deteriorate."

Or, "If only you wouldn't get so hysterical when we discuss our future plans, I would be more willing to share my life with you. I just can't tolerate your emotionalism."

I believed, at the time, that the husband was the captain of the ship. When I gave the orders, I expected everyone to "snap to" and follow my leadership without offering resistance or asking questions. My distorted view made me continually critical of my wife's behavior. I can remember threatening her in a rough tone of voice to emphasize the importance of what I was saying. I gave her the silent treatment, clamming up, hoping to gain her attention so she would come crawling to me after seeing the error of her ways. And I can easily recall my persistence in lecturing her over and over again on the same issues.

Belittling lectures never work with any person, and it's known today to be one of the major reasons for divorce. But the next four suggestions are proven ways to change your wife's behavior — and your own — for the better.

Become a Consistent Example of What You Want Her to Be

Studies have shown that children are much more likely to copy their parents' actions rather than their words. I have found the same principle true in adult relationships. A wife is subconsciously much more willing to emulate her husband's attitudes if they have a good relationship and she admires him. Unfortunately, the converse is true also. The more a husband demands that his wife change when he isn't a good example himself, the less desirous she is to improve herself.

I tried to change my wife in a certain area for months. I bribed her, embarrassed her, threatened not to take her on vacations, and endeavored in many "creative" ways to make her change. But the more I talked, the less she seemed to hear. I finally realized how unloving my attitude had been. I told myself I would not say another word to her about her problems until I could control myself enough to change into the tender and loving husband she needed. I was judging her in the same areas I was guilty (Rom. 2:1–2).

How can a man expect his wife to gain self-control in areas of her life when he does not have it in his own?

Now I was ready to do some changing. "Norma, I've been thinking of trying to change, and I'm ready to start. I'm going to get off your back."

"You know," she said, "I've really been doing some thinking myself, and I really do want to change, especially in that one area that bothers you."

"No, no," I said, "don't do that, because I want to be the first to change. If you change, I won't have as much incentive—you know how competitive I am."

"No, honey, I really want to try harder, and I'm going to change," she replied.

I was so confused because this was the first time she had *ever* been interested in changing. Then she said something I will never forget.

"Gary, you know one of the reasons why it's been so hard for me to break some of my habits? It's because your attitude was so terrible. When you criticized me, I lost all desire and energy to try. And you are so hateful about criticizing me that I didn't want to improve because it would reinforce your stinky attitudes."

Now that I had taken the pressure off, she told me she could sense the difference in my attitude. "Gary, I really want to change, and you're really helping me now."

Do Not Resort to Manipulation or Power Statements

I learned that a husband's tender, sensitive, and understanding attitude creates far more desire within a wife to change than almost anything else he can do. Unfortunately, I hadn't learned the quality of sensitivity during our early years, and because of my manipulations and power statements, my wife did not always feel free to be completely honest with me for fear of my reactions.

A cold chill runs through me when I remember how much it hurt our marriage for Norma to feel she couldn't tell me her true feelings. One of our most painful experiences in this area began at a family reunion.

We were both tired and irritated after a long day at a family get-together near Lake Tahoe when a disagreement began. I don't know how we found enough energy to have such a fight, but it flared quite easily into an argument. I became more irritated and disturbed when she repeatedly refused to submit to me about my change of schedules. Finally her attitude bugged me so much that I told her I had had it. Here I was, on the staff of an organization that taught others how to have family harmony, and I couldn't even achieve it in my own family. I lived with an uneasy feeling that Norma might blow up at the wrong time and embarrass me. I didn't want that pressure anymore, so I decided I had no choice but to quit my job and try a different type of work.

We were both so angry that evening we didn't speak. I woke up at five the next morning with a sick feeling in the pit of my stomach and walked down to the lake to think. I thought through what I would say to my boss and how I would handle the changes about to happen in my life. With a degree of peace, I walked back to the motel to tell Norma of my plans.

She began to cry, begging me not to quit my job. "I was wrong," she sobbed. "I'll change."

Her immediate change in attitude confused me.

"This time you can trust me because I guarantee you this will never happen again as long as we live," she said, still crying. "I really don't want you to quit your job because you will blame me the rest of our lives. Anything you tell me to do, I will do it."

"At last," I thought, "she is beginning to see the error of her ways. Now we can get down to the business of developing a more harmonious marriage."

I couldn't have been further from the truth. Norma had not been completely honest with me. Instead of a change of mind, she was so hurt and offended inside by my critical attitude that her heart had hardened. But since I was threatening her security, to take her away from friends and a home she loved, to move to a different location with no promise we'd even have any money, she hid her true feelings. At that time, I didn't understand how devastating such a threat could be. Norma fought to save her home the only way she knew—by giving in to me. But it wasn't because she suddenly understood my theory of marriage; it was simply that she had no alternative.

To this day, and throughout our forty-five years of marriage, I have struggled with making power statements to my wife whenever she doesn't conform to my ideas. I cannot count the number of times I have threatened to quit the Smalley Relationship Center in an attempt to take control of the marriage. Knowing security is one of Norma's greatest needs, I have often used that to get what I want. But thank God, no more!

I have been learning to apply the greatest truth of my life: I must not control or change anyone but myself, and my happiness is *my* responsibility. My decision to take responsibility for my own heart and to stop trying to change Norma have given me the marriage of my dreams.

Because of my selfish, manipulative behavior, Norma harbored resentful feelings for years. Consequently, our relationship could not become what it should have because of her unspoken resentment toward me. She can remember hating me on the inside but smiling on the outside. It makes me shudder to think about it. Since she appeared happy on the surface, I couldn't sense that she was inwardly disgusted with me.

As I look back on the experience today, I realize where I was at fault. I was demanding and insensitive to her needs. I made no effort to understand her physical and emotional limitations and how sudden changes affect a woman. I was also very critical of her attitudes and her fatigue. I threatened her security in a cold, calculating way. Had I been understanding enough to have waited a day or two to discuss what I wanted to do, the outcome might have been different. Only after I realized the error in my ways did we develop the kind of relationship that allowed Norma to share her feelings honestly with me.

Don't Demand; Share How You Feel

The third way to increase your wife's desire to improve your marriage is to *share* how you feel instead of demanding that she improve. Let me clarify the sharing principle by breaking it down into four parts.

Take a Time-out

If you are angry, wait to share your feelings until your anger has subsided. When you are angry, the tone of your voice alone is likely to provoke the wrong reaction in your wife. You might even spit out words you really don't mean. While you are waiting to cool off, either remain silent or change the subject to a neutral one. If your wife asks why you are quiet, answer her honestly. Try to avoid sarcasm and say something like, "I need a little time to think this through so I can better understand my feelings." Psychologist Henry Brandt encourages a husband and wife to be honest enough to say, "I'm angry right now, and to discuss our problem would be disastrous. Could we wait until I've cooled off?" By waiting, you will be able to have a discussion instead of an argument. Instead of giving the kids a time-out, take one for your marriage. Give yourself time and space to create a safe atmosphere for healthy discussion.

Convey a Loving Attitude

Learn to express your feelings through loving attitudes: warmth, empathy, and sincerity. Loving attitudes dramatically increase a woman's desire to hear your comments. Warmth is the friendly acceptance of a person, the feeling that a person is important enough for your time and effort. Empathy is the ability to understand and identify with your wife's feelings. Can you put yourself in her shoes and see the situation from her vantage point? Sincerity is showing a genuine concern for your wife both in public and at home. A comment such as, "You won't believe my old lady," gives your wife good reason to be an "old lady" when you go home.

Avoid "You" Statements

Try to avoid using "you" statements when sharing your feelings. When you say to your wife, "You never clean up this house," or, "You never have dinner on time," or, "You always yell at the children," you will find she is apt to dig her heels in deeper to resist you. According to psychologist Jerry Day, "you" statements make her more determined to have her own way. When a husband says in anger, "Can't you ever think about my feelings for a change?" she thinks, "His feelings! What about my feelings!" "You" statements seldom make your wife think about you; they usually infuriate her because she knows you're not concerned with her feelings.

Use "I Feel" Statements

Replacing "you" statements with "I feel" messages after you have both cooled down is a better way to share disagreements. Here are a few examples of what I mean:

Areas Your Wife Needs to Improve	Typical "You" Statements to Avoid	Examples of "I Feel" Messages
She doesn't respect you.	"You don't respect me like you should."	"Honey, you probably don't realize how deeply I feel your words, but I really feel discouraged whenever I hear you say disrespectful things to me." (Plug in the statement she uses that discourages you.)
She doesn't accept you the way you are.	"You're always trying to make me into somebody I'm not."	"Honey, I don't blame you for saying a lot of the things you say to me. Many times we're just not in the same world. But I honestly don't understand many of the ways I offend you. And I feel that you're not accepting me for who I am."
She is impatient with you.	"You never give me a chance. Would you get off my back and give me a break? I'm not perfect. I'm not as bad as Sarah's husband."	"Honey, I think you deserve a gold medal for putting up with me, and I wish our relationship were better for your sake. I wish I were more skilled in taking care of you, but it's probably going to take me a long time to learn these new habits. Many times I feel helpless or like a failure. I lose my desire to try when you're critical of me for not improving as fast as you wish I would."

Areas Your Wife Needs to Improve	Typical "You" Statements to Avoid	Examples of "I Feel" Messages
She is critical of you in front of others.	"You make me sick when you criticize me like you did tonight. If you ever say that again I will never take you to another party. You sure made a fool of me tonight."	"Honey, I know how much you enjoy being with our friends. Would there be some time in the near future when we could talk about how I feel when we're at those parties? I hate to bring it up, but there's something you do that dampens my desire to be with our friends together. I really feel embarrassed and low when you criticize me in front of them."

Abandon "I Told You So" Statements

No matter how it's said, if it means "I told you so," eliminate it from your vocabulary. Such statements reflect an arrogance and self-centeredness that can be harmful to your marriage. Here are some of the more typical ways of saying "I told you so":

- "If you had done what I asked you to do in the first place, this wouldn't have happened!"
- "I knew it ... just like I thought. I only asked you to do one thing ... I can't believe that you ... you never listen, do you? ... See-e-e-e-e?"
- "You always have to do it your way, don't you? Well, I hope you're satisfied now."
- "I'm not going to say it but ... maybe someday you'll learn to take my advice."

Can you think of any additional ways that you say to your wife, "I told you so"?

1. _____

2. _____

3. _____

If you can't think of any at the moment, ask your wife if she can remember some of them. Norma could.

I search out the ways I have hurt Norma's feelings, and she does the same with me. She is secure, knowing I won't allow her to mistreat me. She likes to be held accountable for how she makes me feel. I too believe it is important for a husband to have the courage to share his feelings with his wife. A lion can roar and growl, but it takes a real man to say it gently. Tell her you need comfort. Let her know you need praise. (I feel I need the same basic treatment Norma does. If she wants me to improve as a husband, it is essential that she knows what encourages or discourages me in the process.) You are the main one who can tell your wife what you need.

Create Curiosity

Another way to increase your wife's desire to improve comes from the old saying, "You can lead a horse to water but you can't make him drink." But you *can* make him drink if you put salt in his oats. The more salt you put in his oats, the greater his thirst and the more he drinks. The more curious you make your wife, the more she will want to listen. This principle has been aptly named the "salt principle." Be stingy in sharing your feelings. Don't share them with your wife until you have her full attention. Once you master the salt principle, you will be able to gain the attention of anyone, even when he or she knows what you are doing. Simply stated, the principle is this: Never communicate your feelings or information you consider to be important without first creating a burning curiosity within the listener.

The salt principle is so powerful that I can gain the attention of my family even if their eyes are glued to the television. If I want my children to go to bed immediately, I can use the salt principle to get them there without threats, taunts, or screams. Christ left us the example by his method of teaching and motivating people. He used parables to create interest. In fact, he advised us not to teach truth to the uninterested (Matt. 7:6).

The salt principle is so powerful that I have gotten myself into trouble using it. During a speech to a large group, someone asked a question that made me say without thinking, "Do you realize a wife can gain six attitudes that really motivate her husband to want to improve?" The moment those words left my mouth, I realized I was in trouble. A woman's hand went up. "What are those six attitudes?" she asked. I inwardly groaned as I realized I could not discuss those six attitudes and finish the topic I had started. Lowering my head, I apologized to the audience for tantalizing their curiosity. I didn't forget this salt episode because after the meeting I was mobbed by curious women. I can't say I felt like Burt Reynolds, but I did have to spend an hour after the meeting explaining the six attitudes. Now if you're wondering what those six attitudes are, you can find them in the companion to this book, *For Better or for Best*.

Let me use four steps to illustrate how to catch your wife's attention when you want to share your feelings.

First, clearly identify the feeling you wish to communicate to your wife. For example, you want her to understand how discouraged you become when she corrects you in public.

Second, identify some of the areas your wife wants you to change. Perhaps your wife would like you to show affection for her by holding her hand or putting your arm around her in public.

Third, use her area of high interest, salted with just a pinch of your feelings, to stimulate her curiosity. Use her high interest for affection in public and say something like, "Honey, when we're out in public or with our friends, I just want to put my arm around you and show everyone how proud I am of you. But there's something that you do occasionally that takes away my desire to hold you."

And fourth, add a little more salt by asking a short question to further arouse her curiosity. Say something like, "Do you know what you do?" Or, "I probably shouldn't say anything at this time, right?" Or, "Would you be interested in hearing what it is that causes me to feel this way?" If she isn't interested by this time, try it again later. Add a larger dose of salt to your statements. Remember, she may say, "I know what you are doing. It's not going to work this time." Don't believe her, it works when it works! Keep trying it until it does.

Below are four examples of how a husband can "salt" his wife to listen to his feelings.

Area you wish your wife would change	*"Salt" statements that motivate your wife to change*
1. She resists your sexual advances.	"Honey, do you know what really encourages me to make our marriage better? (No.) It's when I see us working together in building our marriage. (Oh, that's good.) I can think of a major area that makes me feel that you're not pulling with me. (Oh, what's that?) Is now a good time to talk about it? (Yes.) Well, I feel misunderstood and rejected when you don't respond to me at night. Could you tell me what's wrong?" *(Be extra gentle and tender during the ensuing discussion. You may find out that she feels offended or any number of possibilities, but you don't have to solve the problem in one discussion. Just listen to deeply understand. Often, that's all she needs.)*

Area you wish your wife would change	*"Salt" statements that motivate your wife to change*
2. She monopolizes the conversation at parties.	"Honey, I know you want to go to their home next week, but there's one thing that keeps happening when we're together that really drives me away from social gatherings in general. (Oh, what is it ... gulp.) Well, I'm not sure I can really explain it without offending you. (Gulp, gulp.) Do you really want to talk about it? (Yes.) Well, I feel left out at parties by you." *(Ask her how both of you could balance this problem. Maybe you could talk a little more and she a little less. If you discuss a plan before going to the party, you will enhance the possibility of it being more enjoyable for both of you.)*
3. She doesn't want to talk when you're alone with her.	"Honey, here we are again, talking about improving our relationship. You still want that, don't you? (Yes.) The best relationship possible that we can build together? (Yes.) There's one thing I don't understand that happens to us during different times of the week, and I think that it is not going to help our relationship, especially after the children are grown and married and we're all alone. (Oh, what's that?) Well, it sort of involves the quiet times when you and I are all by ourselves and I'm really wanting to talk to you, but you don't seem to have this same desire to talk to me. I'm just wondering if there's something I'm doing that I'm not aware of, because I really want to talk to you, but I don't sense that same interest in you.

Area you wish your wife would change	*"Salt" statements that motivate your wife to change*
	Maybe I'm not being sensitive to your fatigue or whatever. I'd just like to know, because I really feel left out when you don't talk to me when we're alone."
4. She nags you about household repairs.	"Honey, I don't blame you for doing one particular thing to me from time to time, because I'm sure I deserve it. But when you say one thing to me it really causes me to lose interest in repairing things around the house. (Oh, what's that?) Well, I know it has something to do with me, and I haven't been able to figure it out yet. But in the meantime, it's not helping me to want to fix things around here. (Well, what is it? Tell me.) Maybe you can help me. Would now be a good time for you to help me figure out why you do this particular thing to me? (Yes, dear, whatever it is, let's get it out in the open and talk about it.) Well, you see, honey, I feel so unmotivated when you, sometimes in irritation or in anger, tell me five times to do something and I just can't remember to do it. As much as I want to, my mind just gets occupied with other things and I just can't remember. I really want to help around the house. How can we figure out together what needs to be done to help me get these things done and help you not to nag me about them? I feel really disinterested in doing it when you're nagging me."

In summary, if a man truly wants his wife to improve and their marriage to be strengthened, he should be the example of what he wants to see in her before saying anything to her. He should be courageous enough to lovingly share his feelings and avoid accusing her. And finally, he should use the salt principle to gain her full attention before sharing his feelings.

For Personal Reflection

1. List the changes you desire in your wife and then write out your own projects to become her example. See Romans 2:1–2; 15:18.

2. Think of some behavior that bothers you, then practice using an "I feel" statement to convey your feelings to your wife in a loving, gentle, understanding way. See Proverbs 15:1.

12

WATCH OUT!
IT CAN HAPPEN TO YOU

■ ■ ■

A man's pride will bring him low,
but a humble spirit will obtain honor.

Proverbs 29:23

"Norma, I really think you should take a couple of days away from the kids considering all you've faced during my absence, all the guests you had to entertain, the wedding shower, painting Greg's room.... I'll get a babysitter, and you just relax. I don't think you're holding up too well." I was trying to get back to work on this book, and somehow it irritated me that Norma sounded nervous and looked uptight.

She said, "I didn't need that. It makes me feel like you don't think I can handle things on my own."

"But I don't think you're handling yourself well," I said with a scowl and a harsh voice. "Surely writing a book involves more pressure than staying with the kids!"

Then the principles in my book flashed before me and broke through my irritation. I realized I was irritated and nervous and that Norma was bearing the brunt of my insensitivity. I had blown it again!

"You're right. You didn't need that. You *are* doing great. When will I ever learn?"

The next morning she came over to my hideaway motel for breakfast, and we again discussed how I had missed a chance to encourage her. My motives were to help, but my insensitive words came out of a doubt that I really was the kind of husband I should be. If I were the right kind of husband, maybe my wife wouldn't have to feel so nervous and rundown. My thoughts had been, "Honey, only a week and I'll be finished with both books. Please hang on. What will people think of my book if you don't look like I'm making you happy?"

Norma said she understood and reminded me that my offensive behavior came less and less often, that the periods of disharmony got shorter and shorter as we learned how to restore our relationship.

Why did those hard times fade away? Two reasons:

1. I *admit* my offensive ways and quickly accept the fact that I haven't arrived.

2. I *earn* her forgiveness sooner by following the ideas in chapter 5.

(And we are both reaching for the best possible relationship. That helps a lot!)

"But," you ask, "when can I relax and enjoy the fruit of my labor?"

Do you remember the story of the young couple who separated for a year until the husband learned how to regain his wife's affection? (See chapter 2.) She couldn't live with his lazy, insensitive, dominant, selfish mannerisms.

He followed many of the principles shared in this book for five years after they reunited, and she was regaining a romantic love and starting to blossom. Then he made the big mistake! He relaxed and wanted a little return for his years of effort. He assumed that now he could start enjoying the fruit of his labor. He slowly reverted to his old habits and attitudes: lazy, insensitive, dominant, selfish. Once again she started to lose her feelings of love for him.

Today he is starting all over again. Fortunately, this time they both desire a better marriage and both are seeking help as a couple.

Building a Successful Marriage Is a Lifelong Endeavor

Don't relax! And never assume that you've arrived! Pride always comes before a fall (Prov. 29:23). Marriages are either growing closer or drifting apart. There is no such thing as a "normal, relaxed marriage." A relationship is dynamic, ever changing, and needs to be nurtured every day just like a vegetable garden. It may not look bad today, but leave it alone for a short time and it takes the same amount of work to bring it back as if I would have spent the small amount of time each day.

You may say, "I'm tired of starting all over again."

One man couldn't stick with it. He kept forgetting some of the principles shared in this book. His wife was ready to leave him, and nothing seemed to help, until one day I said to him, "Jim, each time you fail to comfort her and each time you lose your temper, you're back to the starting block in her mind — at that point she still wants to leave you."

"That does it," he said. "No way am I going to keep starting all over again." And he didn't. That was the end of his angry outbursts.

You may take great strides forward, but each time you slip, your wife may think you haven't changed a bit. Remember, it took my wife two years to believe that I had truly changed. So press forward.

Keep doing the right thing, over and over and over again. And keep in mind the words of Paul:

> Not that I have already obtained all this, or have already arrived at my goal, but I press on to take hold of that for which Christ Jesus took hold of me. Brothers and sisters, I do not consider myself yet to have taken hold of it. But one thing I do: Forgetting what is behind and straining toward what is ahead, I press on toward the goal to win the prize for which God has called me heavenward in Christ Jesus.
>
> All of us, then, who are mature should take such a view of things. And if on some point you think differently, that too God will make clear to you. Only let us live up to what we have already attained.
>
> Philippians 3:12 – 16 NIV

Men, you have not yet been made perfect. But in Christ, you can press on to take hold of a better marriage. With growing maturity, you can live up to what you have already attained. In the words of Winston Churchill, "Never, never, never, never give up" working on your marriage.

For Personal Reflection

1. How does the secret of prayer relate to becoming a more consistently loving husband? See Luke 11:5 – 8 and Luke 18:1 – 7.

2. How many times should a husband forgive his wife and keep trying to build a loving marriage? See Matthew 18:21 – 22.

RESOURCES

Brandt, Henry, with Landrum, Phil. *I Want My Marriage To Be Better.* Grand Rapids: Zondervan, 1976.

Collins, Gary. *How to Be a People Helper.* Santa Ana, Calif.: Vision House, 1976.

Day, Jerry. Clinical Psychologist, Tucson, Arizona: Ideas on stress management.

Dobson, James. *What Wives Wish Their Husbands Knew About Women.* Wheaton, Ill.: Tyndale, 1975.

Drescher, John M. *Seven Things Children Need.* Scottsdale, Penn.: Herald Press, 1976.

Gothard, Bill. Director and lecturer, from the Institute in Basic Youth Conflicts. Oakbrook, Illinois.

Hardisty, Margaret. *Forever My Love.* Irvine, Calif.: Harvest House, 1975.

Hendricks, Howard. *What You Need to Know About Premarital Counseling.* Waco, Tex.: Family Life Cassettes, Word, Inc., 1976.

Hockman, Gloria. "A New Way for Families to Solve Problems Together." *Family Weekly* (July 16, 1978), 6.

Jones, Charles. *Life Is Tremendous.* Wheaton, Ill.: Tyndale, 1968.

LaHaye, Tim and Beverly. *The Act of Marriage.* Grand Rapids: Zondervan, 1970.

LaHaye, Tim. *Understanding the Male Temperament.* Old Tappan, N.J.: Fleming H. Revell, 1977.

Nair, Ken. *Discovering the Mind of a Woman.* Laredo, Texas: Fiesta Publishing Co., 1982.

Osborne, Cecil G. *The Art of Understanding Your Mate.* Grand Rapids: Zondervan, 1970.

Wheat, Ed. Family Physician, Springdale, Arkansas: Tapes on sex in marriage: "Sex Technique and Sex Problems in Marriage," and "Love-Life for Every Married Couple."

RESOURCES BY GARY SMALLEY

The Blessing, coauthored with Dr. John Trent. Nashville: Thomas Nelson, 1986.

Many people spend a lifetime searching for their parents' love and acceptance—their "blessing." *The Blessing* looks at the powerful Old Testament concept of "blessing children" as a tool to help our children in the present and to help us deal with emotional hurts of the past.

For Better or for Best (Revised Edition). Grand Rapids: Zondervan, 1979, 2010.

This book is written just for the wife. Discover practical ways a wife can help to strengthen her marriage and all her important relationships.

The Gift of Honor, coauthored with Dr. John Trent. Nashville: Thomas Nelson, 1987.

Whether we realize it or not, the degree that we value God, others, and ourselves greatly determines the success or failure of all our relationships. Learn what it means to honor God and our loved ones and how to avoid the incredible damage that can come from dishonoring them.

Joy That Lasts. Grand Rapids: Zondervan, 1986.

A personal glimpse into Gary's life as he shares insights from his experience and from the Scriptures—insights that you can use to overcome worry, fear, hurt feelings, anger, and other negative emotions and replace them with love, peace, and joy.

The Key to Your Child's Heart. Waco, Tex.: Word Books, 1984.

Practical parenting methods which have been featured on Dr. Jim Dobson's radio program, "Focus on the Family," including "opening your child's spirit," family contracting, and becoming a close-knit family.

For additional information about Gary's products or his national speaking schedule, please visit us on the web at www.GarySmalley.com.